DABO'S DYNASTY

for Aunt Margie

DABO'S DYNASTY

CLEMSON'S RISE TO
COLLEGE FOOTBALL SUPREMACY

LARRY WILLIAMS

FOREWORD BY TOM RINALDI

THE
History
PRESS

Published by The History Press
Charleston, SC
www.historypress.com

Copyright © 2019 by Larry Williams
All rights reserved

Photographs by Zachary Hanby.

First published 2019

Manufactured in the United States

ISBN 9781467143905

Library of Congress Control Number applied for.

CONTENTS

FOREWORD

In December 2018, my job at ESPN took me to Clemson to report a story on the ten-year anniversary of Dabo Swinney taking over as Clemson's head coach. The story aired the day of Clemson's Cotton Bowl victory over Notre Dame, and the idea was hatched when we saw the series of articles Larry Williams wrote in October for Tigerillustrated.com.

Our story didn't even begin to approach the "Decade of Dabo" series, in which Larry told that story as fully as it deserves to be told. Our story was much shorter due to the time constraints of *College GameDay*; we were just picking a handful of moments between that day in October when Dabo was named the interim coach to the day less than two months later when he was given the job full time. We obviously know what's happened in the aftermath of that decision, but our story just looks at a couple of moments in those seven weeks along that timeline.

I go to school on these coaches I cover and tell stories about, and one of the reasons we are able to is because of people like Larry who write these stories first. When you're able to obtain that kind of content and that kind of insight, it naturally leads to such a strong foundation for us to work off of in terms of what to ask, where to guide the interview and what we can try to do to shape the story in our time constraints of four, five, six minutes long. The series of articles was so revealing and so insightful if you're a storyteller like me. Storytelling is built around anecdote. There's always going to be people who can break down strategy and scheme. There's always going to be people who can give you the Xs and Os. But to me, people remember and relate more to a story. The series by Tigerillustrated.com, whether you're a Clemson fan or not, is so fascinating as a portrait of success. Or the capriciousness, if you will, of what leads to somebody being placed in that position and the other decisions that surround what has turned out to be one of the great decisions—which was to have Dabo Swinney be the head coach of the Clemson Tigers. It is a great case study of how a success happened.

I don't go as far back with Dabo as some other people do. I think I first met him around 2012. This would have been when Clemson was well, well underway in terms of becoming one of the standard-bearers of the sport. So I don't have the depth and length of connection with Dabo that many other people do. But since we've met, I certainly have spent some time with him each of these seasons because of ESPN's deep connection to this sport.

I've covered a lot of unique coaches, but Dabo's program reflects his personality more than any coach I've seen in this sport. Bar none, more than any other coach. The only other team I can think of that reflects the personality of the head coach as much is the Golden State Warriors and Steve Kerr. I cover the NBA at times—nowhere near as much as I cover college football or golf or tennis. But Dabo has built a program in his design, in his image, with his values. And he's been remarkably consistent in doing that.

I think a lot of people wonder about Dabo, whether they say it out loud or not: "Is this guy really this way? Is he too good to be true? Is this an act, or is it authentic?" Certainly, seven years into knowing Dabo, my assessment is that it's completely and totally authentic. And there's reason behind all that he does. A big part of that reason comes from his past experiences and that notebook that he's kept for such a long time that he filled with ideas should he get the opportunity. And he has continued to fill out that notebook and build an incredible program—in his image. I'm eager to see that notebook, but catching him during bowl season when time was at a premium, it wasn't possible during this visit with him.

It's hard to know where to begin when trying to relay the most profound thing I learned about Dabo during this past visit to Clemson and our reporting for this story. One of the most telling moments that Dabo shared with Larry, and with us, was his first action after he got out of Terry Don Phillips's office on October 13. He walked into a storage closet in the facility, called his wife, Kathleen, and then tried to gather himself as best he could and regain his composure. And what did he bring in there with him? That binder. And he began to flood it with more and more ideas—coaching staff, players, fans, training, everything. Because Terry Don told him: "You're empowered. Act like you're the head coach. Do whatever it takes to fix this." He spent half an hour in a storage closet, and within the next half hour he walked to the end of the hall and he fired the offensive coordinator. That tells you something about his confidence and his conviction an hour into receiving the interim tag.

When Dabo went back to that day, he told us he had an overwhelming sick feeling when Terry Don walked into the room with all the coaches and told them Tommy Bowden was gone and Dabo was the interim guy. He didn't use this term with me, but he felt sort of like a dead man walking. When Dabo was the interim coach, the history strongly suggested he would not get the job because it almost never happened like that. Dabo understood that. But it was after that second meeting with Terry Don that Dabo realized he might have a chance. So that one meeting with Terry Don, where the AD told him he believed in him and he wanted him to succeed, how important was that in making Clemson football what it has become? It was seven weeks before the ultimate decision to make Dabo head coach for good.

The vision that he had back then, the vision that he has executed—I don't know that there would be a way to find out whether there has been any coach who has hired more former players on staff, people he has coached or who have been a GA for him, than Dabo. Nineteen—*nineteen*—are on his staff right now. He told me that during our visit. Think about that! That's astounding when you think about the people he brings into his life and keeps in his life. The quality of that connection, the depth of it. I think that says a lot that he had the name Brandon Streeter in that binder years and years ago. Tony Elliott's name, too. The incredible story of how Dabo told Tony that he was going to hire him, where he did—the Sycamore Street part of that, Dabo living on Sycamore Street at the time and Tony having been involved in a traumatic accident where he lost one of his parents on Sycamore in a different part of the country, and him wanting to change the association of that word in Tony Elliott's life. He told Tony about the hiring on Sycamore Street. That is an amazing, amazing anecdote, a window into Dabo.

The television piece that we did on Dabo, while I'm pleased we had the opportunity to do it, is a little less than five minutes long. And one of the big differences in television is that so much that's so wonderful in Dabo's origin story is apocryphal and anecdotal. It's not necessarily visual. So that's a challenge in TV in trying to render that. Dabo is such great TV. He's such a great interview that you keep him on camera a lot. The hardest part of my process by far is pouring my heart and soul into something and then fighting for air time. The two things you want the most are to be accurate and fair.

If that's priority one, then priority 1A is to honor the trust a subject has given. That's what you want. And that's why the battle for time can really be so tough. I'll always believe there's nothing that exists in the realm of objectivity. Because as soon as you select something and omit something else, that's a subjective act. There is no objectivity that's pure and total. But what does exist is sin of omission. And a lot of times I think that's the sin that TV can bring and that I, frankly, commit over and over—the sin of omission, where we're not able to share the story as fully as we'd like to and as fully as Larry did.

A big part of my job of storytelling is earning the trust of the subjects. Two years ago, we came to do the story about Christian Wilkins and the tragic death of his grandfather. For folks who don't know, his grandfather was shot and killed in a mistaken drug raid in Massachusetts. It was a very difficult story to tell. And we did not have a lot of time to tell it with Christian, who is a magnetic, brilliant personality and mind and soul. And really in that case, you have to hope that the connection follows in a way through the interview. But the interview itself ultimately comes down to the quality of the question. Are you prepared and are you asking the right questions? Are you listening to the answers and following up in the right way? That's the ultimate bedrock of a story of that nature. I'm still in touch with Christian, and I see him all the time. I'm still in touch with his mother, who is such a remarkable figure. His whole family story is an incredible portrait of success when you consider secondary collegiate master's degrees all over the family, and he has many siblings who are successful. Obviously, the Campbell Trophy is an incredible feat. But Christian Wilkins and why he wears no. 42, I think that story will forever stand apart for me. It shows his soul and what's important to him.

I think Dabo Swinney and Nick Saban are a lot more similar than people believe. There's no question in my mind. Part of that is their shared authenticity. As different as they are as souls, they are very similar when it comes to being the genuine article. They are who you largely believe they are. That comes from the people who know them and not necessarily the public perception and how that can simplify things. And they get along well, the two of them do. I think there is a great respect between the two of them. I know that Nick Saban has tremendous respect for what Dabo Swinney has built. And we all know what Swinney has said and how he feels about Saban and the program being the standard and the Rest of Y'all Bus and all of that. So I think there's a lot that is shared between them. And one thing: even though Saban is a decade and a half older than Dabo, he hasn't shown any sign of his passion waning. Certainly not that I see. And one of the first places you see it and you know it is in recruiting. And boy, Nick Saban still really gets out there and actually enjoys recruiting.

The difference between the two is the environments inside their football buildings. Saban's rooms and hallways are a pressurized environment, and you can feel the tension. You walk in there, and everything is pressurized. And typically that's not a good thing. The thought in any management book you'd ever read is that people do not operate best under tension. I would ask anyone who has written that line or subscribes to that philosophy—which seems to make a lot of sense—to understand what a contradiction to that Alabama is with its success. A lot is demanded. You can say that tension comes from the unexpected. If that is the case, it's not a tense place. You know exactly what to expect when you walk into that building at Alabama. And you're expected to deliver. And if you don't, you'll be held accountable until you do. And that goes for every single person's task in that building. They celebrate. They have fun. But no one has as much fun that I've seen, in the way that he does, as Dabo Swinney. Now Nick does bring the freshmen out to the lake house during the summer. He drags them on the innertube, as we showed on the "Training Days" series, and they have a lot of fun. And that's a part of him that people don't get to see as often. They see it all the time with Dabo.

I don't think there's any doubt that Saban's effort to bring to light these more fun elements of himself is a reaction to the perception of Dabo and Clemson being a more fun place to be. Saban is aware of the greater landscape. And again, I think that's humility. That is awareness. It's not: "We do it the way we do it, and everyone else and everything else be damned." That is not Nick's way. He appreciates, studies, understands context. And adapts to it. And now he's probably asking himself how he needs to further adapt after Clemson did what it did to Alabama in Santa Clara.

The most remarkable thing about the dominance of Dabo Swinney and Nick Saban is how they have successfully combated the natural reactions to high achievement—there's disharmony, there's turbulence, there's injury, there's self-interest. There are all these things that are enemies to unity and sustained excellence. That's what's so astounding about Dabo and Saban—that they have found a way to defeat that. That's incredible.

One of the things that Saban said and Dabo echoed: there's a lot of books that tell you how to be successful. There are hardly any that tell you how to stay that way.

—Tom Rinaldi

ACKNOWLEDGEMENTS

In December 2007, Dabo Swinney was a Clemson receivers coach preparing for a game in the Chick-fil-A Bowl against Auburn.

A few days before the game in Atlanta, our paths crossed at the Marriott Marquis hotel. Swinney mentioned that one of his brothers was going through some struggles. That began an hour-long conversation in which he shared the story of his difficult upbringing in Pelham, Alabama.

The story is well known now—the alcoholic father whose demons left the family homeless at one point, Swinney's mother having nowhere else to go but her son's apartment when he was at Alabama and plenty of other difficult circumstances—but back then it had yet to be publicized.

At the time, I just assumed Swinney wanted that story private. But less than a year later, he became interim head coach at Clemson, and I took a shot at asking him if he was willing to go on the record with it.

"Sure," he said. And so we sat for hours at different times as he shared all the trauma and turmoil and hard times that made him the man he was and is. The man who at the time was also trying to win over a team, a fan base, an administration.

Ten years later, another idea came to mind. What if Swinney went over to the old football offices, the McFadden Building, where his life—and the life of Clemson football—was forever changed on that day of October 13, 2008? What if he retraced his steps and his thoughts from that day and we recorded it for a video that would run on that exact day ten years later? This idea was presented to him early in the season when he was managing a high-profile quarterback battle, among plenty of other things. So it would have been completely understandable had he said he was too busy and declined.

He liked the idea and again said, "Sure." And sure enough, a few weeks later, he showed up to spend considerable time unearthing all those memories and walking through those same hallways and doorways, reviving a time when he was just some receivers coach with a strange first name people were still wondering how to pronounce. The two-part video closed a weeklong series of articles we published at Tigerillustrated.com commemorating a decade of Dabo.

In February 2016, I wrote the book *Clemson Tough: Guts and Glory Under Dabo Swinney*. It was less about that breakthrough 2015 season and more about how Swinney built the program to the point of being fit to compete against anyone and everyone—even Alabama in the national championship. So even though they lost to Alabama that first time, even though they closed the deal a year later on that unforgettable night in Tampa, the book still held up because it was about the foundations. And a big reason for that was Swinney's willingness to be himself, to expand on topics and ideas and be open to exploring those foundations.

This book came together quickly. The week Clemson traveled to Santa Clara to play Alabama for the national title, Chad Rhoad of The History Press reached out to gauge interest in a work on the 2018 season. I told him if the Tigers beat Alabama, I was in. So two days after Clemson concluded a dismantling that shook college football to its core, work began. Seven days later, these are the final words being typed before the manuscript is submitted.

Plenty of the content in this work consists of ideas and themes that I explored during the season for my job at Tigerillustrated.com and then fleshed out. The "Decade of Dabo" series from October was perfect to build upon and then sprinkle into the story of this team. They are flashbacks to the pivotal, almost mystical junctures from the more distant past—important layers of context and anecdote that explain and underpin the journey from 2008 to now.

Thank you to photographer Zachary Hanby for sharing his fine work for this book. If you like his photos and would like to see more, shoot him an e-mail at Zachary@zachphoto.net. Thank you to friend Ben Long of Blind Moose Media, a Clemson grad who produced outstanding work as the videographer of Swinney's walk down memory lane. Thank you to friends Gene Sapakoff, Ron Morris, David Hale and Doug Hayes for reading through the first draft of the manuscript and offering great advice.

ACKNOWLEDGEMENTS

Thank you to Clemson's assistant coaches, particularly Tony Elliott, Jeff Scott and Brent Venables, for being so patient in helping me better understand what I was covering. Thank you to the players for showing up to a seemingly endless procession of interviews featuring a seemingly endless procession of the same questions.

Thank you to ESPN's Tom Rinaldi for being exceedingly gracious and eager to provide the foreword for this book.

Thank you to my wife for her guidance and unwavering support. Thank you to my two girls for their patience upon my arrival home from Santa Clara. Months of nonstop work was supposed to be over when the season was over, and then they were informed one more week of nonstop work was commencing once Dad stepped back in the door.

Most of all, thanks to Dabo for allowing great stories to be told. Without his decision to make his life and himself and his program an open book, works like this don't happen. Without his answers of "Sure" to deeper story ideas in 2008, 2018 and plenty in between, he's just another coach presiding over just another dominant football program.

One anecdote from hours after the national championship game: Swinney had done the celebrating on the field and in the locker room. He had taken part in media obligations here, there and everywhere. He was finally with his family now in the quiet corridors of Levi's Stadium, heading back to an empty locker room after everyone else had headed to the buses.

Dabo, his wife, Kathleen, and other family members decided to take a quick detour back to the field. They were going to do snow angels—make that confetti angels—in orange and purple paper that had fallen from the skies earlier when the Alabama fans were long gone and the Clemson fans were beside themselves with joy.

Speaking of joy: Swinney always comes up with one word that will carry him and his team through a season, and that's the word he chose for 2018.

That's what pushed him, in an action uncharacteristic of most coaches in his tax bracket, to go back onto that field and celebrate like a child with loved ones.

And, indirectly, it's what pushes stories like this to be told to you.

—Larry Williams
January 15, 2019

INTRODUCTION

I n March 2003, Bill D'Andrea got a call from Danny Pearman. The two had been together at Clemson in the 1980s when D'Andrea was a coach and Pearman a player. Now Pearman was an assistant at Virginia Tech, and he was calling D'Andrea to tell him about a new guy who was interviewing for a job coaching the Tigers' receivers.

That was the first time D'Andrea, then Clemson's senior associate athletics director, heard the name Dabo Swinney. On that interview, first-year athletics director Terry Don Phillips wanted D'Andrea to spend a few minutes chatting with Swinney. Pearman, who was with Swinney at Alabama for eight years when Swinney was a player and then a coach, told D'Andrea about Swinney and his family. He said he was there when Swinney's first son, Will, was born.

And as you'd expect, it didn't take long in that initial meeting for D'Andrea to observe that there was just something different about this thirty-three-year-old guy who was getting back into coaching. "Dabo just had an engaging personality," D'Andrea said. "He was giving up a pretty lucrative job in real-estate development. He knew he wanted to coach. It was his calling. It was a brief interview, kind of chatting back and forth about who knew who. Terry Don, for some special reason, had his eye on Dabo ever since he came here."

These little snapshots, which didn't seem all that important at the time, have such gravity now as we think back to all the things that had to fall into place for this incredible, irresistible story to happen. Why yes, it's been ten seasons. A decade of Dabo that began on an October day when Tommy

Bowden decided he didn't want to continue coaching, knowing he'd have to win the ACC's Atlantic Division to keep his job. And sixteen years since Swinney, who'd spent almost two years selling commercial real estate after Mike DuBose's staff was fired at Alabama, came to Clemson when Bowden made what seemed a bizarre hire of a receivers coach.

D'Andrea was Phillips's right-hand man on coaching searches, a sounding board and confidant when important decisions were being made. He was the man who put that orange jacket onto Swinney's shoulders in December 2008 when the interim tag was stripped from Swinney's title, two days after the Tigers beat up Steve Spurrier's South Carolina Gamecocks in what has to go down among the most important victories in school history.

D'Andrea, who like Phillips remains in the Clemson area, remembers the coaching search Phillips conducted while Swinney was auditioning for the job. He remembers names like Gary Patterson, Will Muschamp, Lane Kiffin, Brent Venables and Bud Foster. He remembers a lot of names that made more conventional sense than handing the reins to a guy who'd never even run an offense. Phillips's fascination with Swinney long predated that period in 2008 when Swinney was trying to galvanize a program, a fan base, a culture. Years earlier, the reserved Phillips had begun to observe Swinney and his magnetic aura.

"A lot of times I'd go to Terry Don's office late in the afternoon and I'd ask him if he wanted to go out to watch practice," D'Andrea said. "Sometimes we would go out together. But if he wasn't going to go and had something to do, he would say: 'Make sure you look over there and watch the receivers and watch Dabo.' I look back at those comments and I think Terry Don really knew that Dabo was special. He had that authenticity and that sincerity. He got on his kids when they didn't do him right. But he also hugged them up. I'm sure Dabo knows Xs and Os, but he has that special category of caring for people—a care that's just broader than football."

Fan morale was in the ditch in October 2008. A 12–7 loss at Wake Forest on a Thursday night dropped the Tigers' record to 3-3. A season-opening curb-stomping at the hands of Alabama and a home loss to Maryland made a mockery of the Top 10 ranking Clemson carried into the season. This program, which had won a national title in 1981 and collected a long list of big-name wins under Charley Pell and Danny Ford in the late 1970s and 1980s, had been wandering around in the wilderness for almost two decades. And now people were fed up with Bowden, who was supposed to break through in his tenth season but ended up breaking down instead. Over Bowden's tenure, the Tigers could beat almost anyone but also lose to almost anyone—sometimes in back-to-back games.

Swinney was far from the obvious choice. He was an obscure name even to many of Clemson's own fans, and there were two former head coaches on staff in Brad Scott and Vic Koenning. The previous season, Bowden had flirted seriously with Arkansas. Phillips ended up working out an extension to keep Bowden from getting on that plane to Fayetteville, but afterward, he told this writer he would have strongly considered a Clemson assistant had Bowden left.

It was assumed he meant one of the coaches who had experience running a program, probably Koenning. Nope. He was thinking big about Swinney even then. The man who years earlier had identified Les Miles and Mike Gundy as head coaches viewed Swinney as another diamond in the rough.

Less than a year later: "Here we were, hiring a coach that wasn't even a coordinator," D'Andrea said. "There were a lot of people in IPTAY that had e-mailed me saying they were leaving because we were making a bad decision. He didn't have the experience."

Even on an interim basis, when he was guaranteed nothing beyond the final six games of the regular season, Swinney made a priority of connecting with fans in ways that Bowden had not. The first Tiger Walk, which has become ingrained as a celebrated pregame ritual, was before Swinney's first game against Georgia Tech. He invited students to come watch practice and even allowed some to participate. When fans wrote to him offering their support, somehow he found the time to write back thanking them. He told them how much he loved the passion of Clemson fans, told them it was a privilege to lead the program. He told them better days were ahead for the Tigers.

Clemson seemed a galaxy away from 1981. Even ten-win seasons and ACC titles seemed like fantasy as Virginia Tech dominated the ACC and the Tigers watched Boston College and Wake Forest parade to the conference championship game as the Atlantic Division representatives. But Swinney knew how to speak the fans' language, knew how to connect, from the very beginning.

"Dabo was inclusive," D'Andrea said. "He brought the institution together. He invited faculty to practice. He brought the band out there. He just did things that—some people might view it as a marketing opportunity, but those were things we needed at that time. There were a lot of people who were disappointed."

In a short time, Swinney connected with supporters in a way that Bowden never did in nine-plus seasons. Clemson fans want someone they can reach out and touch and relate to. Bowden, who upon his hire at Clemson was hailed as the second coming of his father, the folksy, charismatic Florida State legend Bobby Bowden, just wasn't that type of guy. He never seemed to let his guard down. His successor never seemed to have his up.

"I think Tommy Bowden is a good person and a good coach," D'Andrea said. "He certainly came from a good family with his father being successful. I think he knew about recruiting. I think he knew about family. But there was some element he was missing. He just wasn't as sincere and authentic as Dabo was or as some of the other coaches I knew. There were a lot of complaints from donors, not so much that they didn't like Tommy. It was that Tommy always appeared to have somewhat—he didn't take the blame. It was, 'We didn't make a first down,' or 'We missed a kick,' or 'Two plays away.' I think most CEOs in leadership positions, when they have that responsibility, they take that ownership. I sensed that he knew he was responsible, but what I think he needed to do is come out and tell the fans: 'The buck stops here with me.' I think he had a hard time sharing that. Dabo is able to reach down and touch your soul. Where Tommy was only able to touch the skin."

D'Andrea said one of the first moves Swinney wanted to make upon getting the job was hiring away Ellis Johnson from South Carolina. Swinney and Koenning did not have a good relationship, and Swinney had long been close with Johnson. D'Andrea called South Carolina to ask about Johnson's contract and was informed the buyout was $500,000. That was too steep for Clemson, so Swinney then pursued John Chavis but lost him when LSU paid him big money Clemson couldn't match. Kevin Steele ended up coming to Clemson, and that marriage seldom seemed to work well over Steele's three-year tenure. So a lot has changed, because at the moment there's no way Clemson would let half a million bucks get in the way of a coach Swinney wanted. Venables, arguably the top assistant in college football, has been at Clemson for seven years after leaving Oklahoma and is earning more than $2 million a year.

In January 2006, D'Andrea was on the university plane with Swinney and running backs coach Burton Burns. Southern Cal was a giant in those days, and Reggie Bush was a force-of-nature running back for the Trojans. "Y'all need to go get a tailback like Reggie Bush," D'Andrea told Swinney and Burns. Their reply: "Oh, we've got one."

That was the first time D'Andrea heard the name C.J. Spiller. Swinney was solely responsible for selling Spiller on the notion of simply going to Clemson for a visit, let alone signing with the Tigers. Without Spiller, maybe Bowden is gone sooner. Without Spiller, where is Swinney in October 2008? Where is Clemson now? The what-ifs sort of take your breath away, don't they?

D'Andrea remembers hopping on the team buses for a road trip during Swinney's audition. One of Swinney's new rules was everyone had to dress to the nines when the team traveled. No more warm-ups or sweatpants or whatever else the team was wearing before he took over. Swinney was going to go out doing it his way, and a big part of that was first-class representation of the football program. Phillips and D'Andrea were sitting near the front of the first bus when the head coach walked up the stairs. He was followed by his wife, Kathleen, and their three boys. Phillips leaned over to D'Andrea and said, "Look at that beautiful family."

Look at this beautiful decade. A decade of Dabo. Ten seasons that culminated with a confirmation of Dabo's Dynasty.

D'Andrea: "There was just something that gravitated Terry Don to Dabo, whether it was divine intervention or what."

CHAPTER 1

SUPERDOME DOOM

I
t was easy, too easy, to think that Clemson's time to eclipse Alabama's dynasty would come on January 1, 2018, in New Orleans. That was a popular narrative entering the College Football Playoff semifinal at the Sugar Bowl, otherwise known as Round 3 of this captivating postseason ritual between the Tigers and Crimson Tide.

Alabama had looked awful its last time out in a loss at Auburn, a defeat that put Nick Saban's program on the dangerous precipice of not making the playoff field. The Tide managed to get in as a No. 4 seed, a controversial inclusion given that they didn't win their division, let alone conference.

Clemson, meanwhile, was rolling right along without Deshaun Watson, Mike Williams and other transcendent offensive playmakers who had made the difference in the classic triumph over the Saban monster a year earlier in Tampa. The Tigers had suffered a startling setback in a regular-season loss at Syracuse, during which starting quarterback Kelly Bryant left the game with injury, but they were back to late-season destruction mode with a spanking of a ranked South Carolina team in Columbia and a complete dismantling of Top 10 Miami and its turnover chains in the ACC championship game. The Tigers were the No. 1 seed and full of confidence. The Tide were fortunate to be there after looking so bad against Auburn their last time out. Even though Clemson was a slight underdog by the oddsmakers, this was the Tigers' time to snatch the torch of supremacy from a wobbly Alabama program that couldn't figure out how to move the ball and score points.

Kelly Bryant gets hit by Alabama's Anfernee Jennings, and the ball lands in the hands of Da'Ron Payne. Clemson was down 10–6 and driving but was soon in a 17–6 hole after the Crimson Tide converted the interception into a touchdown.

It all made so much sense—until the ball was kicked off at a rowdy Superdome and Trevon Diggs knocked freshman return man Travis Etienne all the way to Bourbon Street. In reality, this was the perfect time for Saban to remind the college football world that he and Alabama weren't going anywhere—except to Atlanta for another trip to the national title game in an all-SEC final against Georgia.

While plenty of outsiders were forecasting their demise in the Sugar Bowl, the Crimson Tide privately stewed for a month. Maybe everyone should have paid closer attention to that part of the storyline. Including Clemson's football team. In the run-up to the game, the solemn, edgy nature of Alabama's players stood in stark contrast to the bouncy, giddy vibe of their Clemson counterparts. A few days before, Tide running back Damien Harris drew surprised stares from reporters when he informed them he didn't explore New Orleans the night before. He was asked if it was because of the frigid temperatures. "No," he replied. "It's because I'm focused on playing Clemson."

Clemson players were all over town, on Bourbon Street and in the casinos. Alabama players were almost nowhere to be found after sundown. It's never been the nature of Clemson's program for players to hole up in their hotel rooms at bowl sites, to not have any fun. And they've kicked plenty of tail in the postseason after enjoying themselves leading up to the game. But this team seemed a little too impressed with itself as it prepared for a showdown with an angry bunch of Alabama players who'd fallen one second short of a national title the year before in a 35–31 defeat. "We had a little bit too much fun in Louisiana," defensive tackle Dexter Lawrence observed later.

Tight end/fullback Garrett Williams said the feel was different from the year before, when the Tigers spent the entire year living with a 45–40 loss to Alabama in the national title game.

"I honestly think they wanted that game more. They had a look in their eye that we might not have had. I think maybe we were a little distracted at points during the week, and it showed in the game, unfortunately. It just seemed like as a group, for some reason we didn't have it. It didn't seem like we had that locked-in mindset quite as much as the year before that."

Human nature is often the most difficult opponent for ultra-successful programs. Saban and Dabo Swinney have done a masterful job of stockpiling talent year after year. But the most remarkable accomplishment for both of them is keeping their players driven and hungry in the presence of rich success. When his team was pursuing its second consecutive national title in 2012, Saban shared some wisdom from Michael Jordan with his players.

"Everybody thinks the first championship is the hardest," Saban quoted Jordan saying. "But it's really the next one, because you have to have the will to fight against yourself, to be everything that you can be because you want to be it, because you've already won a championship."

In 2016, Clemson had generational offensive talents in its favor when it took on Alabama in Tampa. Saban just never could get a handle on Watson in the two title-game meetings, and not even some of the most decorated defensive backs in college football could stick with Williams, Hunter Renfrow or Jordan Leggett over the entire game in Tampa. But what the Tigers really had going for them in 2016 was what happened in 2015. They outplayed Alabama in Glendale. Watson made Saban want to pull his hair out. But they lost because they couldn't take care of details like recovering an onside kick, covering a kickoff or covering a tight end. For an entire year, that stung. And such a sting motivates to no end.

As exhilarating as it was for Clemson to win a national championship with one second on the clock on January 9, 2017, there was also a team that lost a national championship with one second on the clock. Alabama had to deal with that. And then Alabama had to deal with looking awful against Auburn and hearing all that Clemson talk all through December, how the Tigers were eclipsing the Tide. Clemson wasn't supposed to be back in the playoff in 2017 after losing all those offensive playmakers. A third consecutive trip to the CFP while they were rebuilding on that side of the ball sent the message that the Tigers were here to stay. Fans were giddy at the thought of advancing past the semifinal and playing for another national title against either Georgia or Oklahoma. The championship game would be staged in Atlanta, in Clemson's backyard. Could it get any better? Plenty of fans were finding it hard to focus totally on the game, and Renfrow said the same was probably true of the players. It's a major challenge for any elite team to keep the edge amid all the winning and accolades and other teams circling you on their calendar. And the emotional disparity was plain to see on this night against an agitated Alabama team that brought everything it had for what was being billed as "The Trilogy."

"I felt like the bowl prep was about normal," Renfrow said. "But normal wasn't good enough, I guess. I feel like the biggest difference was just on game day. We just didn't have it. We just didn't have what Coach Swinney talks about, the eye of the Tiger. I feel like we prepared well. But we just didn't have that 'it' factor, I guess. That's something that we can learn from so that everything building up from the bowl site, everything we do, is geared toward game day."

From Diggs's smoking of Etienne on the opening kickoff, the tone was set. From that point forward, it was clear this was Angry Alabama and Clemson wasn't going to be able to match the Tide's intensity and vengefulness. They were pissed. And the Tigers seemed almost stunned that they were pissed. In 2015, Clemson piled up 40 points and 550 yards on 85 plays against Alabama. A year later, the Tigers had 35 points, 511 yards and 99 plays. In this game, they didn't reach the end zone once and produced a mere 188 yards in the 24–6 defeat.

Clemson's defense did its job in holding Alabama's offense to 17 points and 261 yards. But the Tigers had terrible field position for most of the game and couldn't make the type of game-changing plays in the passing game that are necessary to beating the Crimson Tide. Receiver Deon Cain dropped several passes, including one Alabama took back for a touchdown. The offensive line was whipped, and Bryant didn't make the Tide fear the downfield passing game the way Watson had in the previous two meetings. Young offensive lineman John Simpson didn't play a snap that night. At one point, line coach Robbie Caldwell motioned for Simpson to go in but then thought better of it and said, "Nah, you're not ready for this."

Defensive end Austin Bryant is dejected in the locker room after a 24–6 loss to Alabama in the Sugar Bowl. Clemson held Alabama's offense to 17 points and 261 yards.

"We were ready for football; they were ready for a fistfight," Simpson said. "It was two different games being played."

Alabama reasserted its dominance, and skeptics of Clemson revived the notion that the Tigers' national title the year before was built on the otherworldly talents of Watson. He was gone now, and there was no way Swinney's program was going to be able to hang with the Saban colossus without a similar presence at quarterback. Casual observers probably didn't notice there was already one of those quarterbacks on campus.

"I tell our guys all the time, it's always about what's next," a dejected Swinney said in his postgame press conference. "We're going to learn and we're going to grow and we're going to always get better. My expectation is to be right back here next year, right back in the middle of it, right back in the thick of it.…I don't think this will be the last one. We'll see. Everybody talks about 'The Trilogy' and all that like somebody's fixing to die or something, like the world is coming to an end. We'll be back. And so will they. We'll have probably several more opportunities to hook it up with these guys. And we look forward to that."

CHAPTER 2

HERE COMES SUNSHINE

Seven days after Clemson fell apart in New Orleans, a seemingly seismic event unfolded in Atlanta at halftime of the national championship game. Alabama coach Nick Saban had entered the Sugar Bowl with plans to insert freshman quarterback Tua Tagovailoa if things started to get dicey against the Tigers. That never happened because Clemson's offense couldn't do much of anything. But at halftime against Georgia, the Crimson Tide were down 13–0 and in desperation mode.

Tagovailoa, a decorated talent from Hawaii, had privately shredded Alabama's first-string defense during practices for the Sugar Bowl when starter Jalen Hurts was out sick. And everything changed for the Tide's offense when he came out for the second half at Mercedes-Benz Stadium. Alabama's offense jolted to life as he spread the ball around to different receivers who suddenly had a new bounce in their steps. In overtime, Tagovailoa ended the game on a breathtaking 41-yard strike to DeVonta Smith.

As Clemson fans watched all this unfold, it was impossible to ignore the parallel with the Tigers' situation. Kelly Bryant, the man who replaced Deshaun Watson, was good enough to get this program to the playoff. But was he good enough for the Tigers to close the deal once there?

A mere year after saying goodbye to the best player in school history, Clemson welcomed another transcendent talent when Trevor Lawrence enrolled early in January 2018. Lawrence broke all of Watson's high school records in the state of Georgia and became a celebrity in Cartersville, a suburb northwest of Atlanta.

The lack of a fearsome downfield passing game was the major factor in Clemson's loss to Alabama in the Sugar Bowl. The addition of one was going to be necessary for the Tigers to chase another national title, and Lawrence had all the tools to do it. In 2014, Watson showed it was possible for a gifted quarterback to do big things a year removed from high school. Now, another freshman was the catalyst in Alabama claiming its fifth national title in nine years.

Bryant had done plenty to earn the respect of his coaches and teammates. Succeeding Watson was an almost impossible task because everything he did was compared to one of the most dynamic dual-threat weapons in college football history. So even if the 2017 team leaned hard on its defense as the offense found its way, Bryant was a high achiever in playing a major role in the Tigers totaling twelve wins, another ACC title and another trip to the playoff.

But the coaches knew how much of a game-changer Lawrence could be. He was so advanced as a passer and made everything look so effortless that it was hard to imagine him lurking in the background for long. Clemson had some decorated quarterbacks on the roster, most notably former five-star Hunter Johnson and also former Elite 11 participant Zerrick Cooper. And Bryant was only going to get better as a senior after his first season as the starter. Nonetheless, the vibe coming out of the football offices in 2017 was that Clemson's best quarterback was playing high school ball in Cartersville. Even that December, when Dabo Swinney officially welcomed Lawrence as a member of the 2018 signing class, the head coach made no attempt to dispel the hype and anticipation.

"He's just so physically developed for a young guy. Deshaun was obviously pretty special coming out of Georgia. He's just way ahead of Deshaun from a physical standpoint. We'll see where he is mentally and how he transitions and all that once he gets here and we start coaching him. I don't know that you really know that until you start coaching a guy, but he's been well prepared and well groomed. He's got everything that you look for, that you could possibly want. He's just been a natural from day one, all the way from ninth grade on. He's got unbelievable arm talent. That's pretty easy to see when you watch him. But I think he's just a very poised guy that is a great competitor. He's been a great leader for his program. He's a very good student and just a guy that I think knows what he wants and is willing to work for it."

Before Lawrence even arrived on campus, Swinney was saying game-on for the 2018 quarterback competition. Lawrence had committed a year earlier, in December 2016, when Watson and the Tigers were preparing for round two against Alabama, and he never remotely wavered.

"We've got good players here," Swinney said. "They all understand competition....Trevor has known what he wants to do, and he's excited about having an opportunity to come in here and compete. My job is to go recruit the best players that I can recruit for Clemson University, and then when they get here challenge them, grow them, mature them, develop them into being the best version of themselves. Competition is going to bring out the best in everyone. And at the end of the day, somebody's going to win the job. You're going to have starters. You're going to have backups. And that's life. That's the way it is. So we have a process in place. You go through it and let the chips fall where they may."

In mid-January 2018, Lawrence was but one of the reasons Clemson fans were able to move on quickly from the demoralization of the Sugar Bowl. For much of 2017, it seemed a foregone conclusion that the defensive line was going to suffer major attrition. Draft-eligible underclassmen Christian Wilkins, Clelin Ferrell and Austin Bryant were considered future pros, and it seemed likely two of the three would go to the NFL and highly plausible that all three would be gone. All three chose to return, giving Clemson an absurd collection of defensive line talent in 2018. They would rejoin junior tackle Dexter Lawrence to form one of the more terrifying defensive lines in college football history. Most NFL-worthy underclassmen have the itch to leave. These pillars of the program had the itch to stay and make right what went wrong in the Sugar Bowl.

But 2017 was proof that a great defense alone wasn't enough to bring home another national championship. The Tigers also needed to score points, and there was a feeling in the football offices that this machine was going to be lethal again in year four under the leadership of co–offensive coordinators Tony Elliott and Jeff Scott. Years earlier, when rock-star coordinator Chad Morris was guiding Clemson's high-flying offenses, fans regularly fretted over what might happen when he left. Swinney laughed at the idea that anything would change, saying at one point in 2012 that this was the Clemson offense and not the Chad Morris offense.

Morris departed for the head-coaching job at Southern Methodist University in December 2014. Instead of taking the big money he was paying Morris and hiring a seasoned play-caller from elsewhere, Swinney made the unconventional move of promoting Elliott (running backs) and

Clemson's starting defensive line was regarded as one of the most decorated in college football history thanks to the return of Clelin Ferrell (99), Christian Wilkins (42) and Austin Bryant (7), who rejoined junior Dexter Lawrence (90).

Scott (receivers) to run the operation. Their first test came a few weeks later in the Russell Athletic Bowl, where the Tigers smoked Oklahoma 40–6. A year later, the Tigers were unstoppable in a 14-0 run to the national title game before special teams and defense ended up being the defining deficiencies in a narrow loss to Alabama. A dip came in 2017, and it was more than understandable given what the offense lost. Scoring 33.3 points per game and rushing for an average of almost 200 was pretty good. It just wasn't good enough to get back to the national title game.

The addition of Trevor Lawrence wasn't the only reason coaches were excited about offensive rejuvenation in 2018. Tee Higgins had star written all over him during some big moments late in his freshman year. Amari Rodgers also showed promise as a freshman in 2017. Hunter Renfrow was back for one more ride. And the 2018 recruiting class included the top player in Alabama (Justyn Ross) and the top player in South Carolina (Derion Kendrick). The Tigers were so loaded at receiver that the coaches didn't really stress much at all when Deon Cain and Ray-Ray McCloud, two former five-star talents, decided to turn pro early after the Sugar Bowl.

Before he even strapped on a Clemson helmet, Lawrence was a sensation when he arrived and began classes. One evening in January, the presence of the six-foot-five figure with the long blond hair in a downtown coffee shop provoked screams from females. Pretty soon, teammates would begin calling him "Sunshine" in reference to the main character in the movie *Remember the Titans*. Cooper, Kelly Bryant's backup in 2017 as a redshirt freshman, announced plans to transfer in mid-January. Another quarterback, Tucker Israel, also left the team. It was reasonable to wonder whether Johnson, who had signed a year earlier, might also be mulling a transfer.

Once spring practice began, it didn't take long for the new guy to give the offense a new dimension. It was a lot like Watson four years earlier when he arrived early and showed the advancement and poise of a junior or senior, not a freshman. Swinney later said Lawrence affirmed everything the staff thought about him on the very first day.

"As a coach, you have a plan for what we call installation: day one install, day two, day three, day four, day five, and you're trying to teach everyone your system. His ability to absorb everything, first of all. So his mind. But then the first day, his skill on the field and watching how he just—he didn't look like a freshman. And that's exactly how Deshaun was. The biggest difference was Deshaun was about 180 pounds when he got there in January and Trevor was probably 205. So physically he was a little bit ahead. But just his demeanor, his poise, his ability to absorb the playbook. I knew pretty early: 'Man, this kid is going to be special.'"

Scott, Elliott and quarterbacks coach Brandon Streeter regularly take jogs during their lunch breaks. In the surreal afterglow of the 2016 national title, on those runs they agreed that it might be a long time before they'd get another one like Watson. As it turned out, it only took a year. As it turned out, Clemson's generational quarterbacks are *re*generational.

"For us to have two guys within a couple of years is really just amazing," Scott said. "They're similar in a lot of ways. Obviously they have a few differences. But for us, it's not just the arm strength. I think it's what you get in meetings when you're sitting down. That was one thing we were probably most impressed with with Trevor. We knew the arm strength. You really don't know how he processes things until you get in a meeting room with him. I can remember really our first week meeting with him, it was like, 'Wow, this guy has a great knowledge already, great foundation, came from a great program there. Joey King, his head coach, one of the best high school coaches in the country. Runs a very similar system.' Trevor during lunch would go to his coach's office, and they'd sit there and watch film. The foundation when he came really helped. What I appreciated about Deshaun was if somebody got him one time with something—a certain look, a certain blitz, disguise—you weren't going to get him on that twice. Once he saw it, he understood it. He could recognize it. We saw a lot of those similarities with Trevor as a young player. It's hard to get him twice. He's able to learn and adapt very quickly."

Even as Bryant played well during spring practice, even as he continued as one of the most popular and beloved figures on the team, it was hard for players to take their eyes off Lawrence. Almost all of the practices are closed to the media, but that didn't keep a steady stream of raves from leaking out. This freshman was doing eye-opening things. Crazy things. Several weeks in, several observers were consulted on the most memorable things they'd seen from no. 16 to that point.

Safety Tanner Muse:

If you just dial in watching him throw, you can definitely see a little difference. Like today, he ran a boot, and he freaking just throws a dart right in there. He was rolling out and there were guys diving. He just put it right in the pocket. There's only these little holes there, and he'll hit them. Or if we're in Cover 2, I'll be coming around and the corner will jam. He'll hit it right in that little hole on the corner routes. There's always those little holes in a defense, and he'll find them sometimes. Even when you're across the field on the opposite hash, you never want to leave your guy if it's a scramble. Because it's probably going to go up, and it's probably going to be your guy. It's good to watch him, his vantage point, because he does have those little freshman vibes where he maybe stares a little bit so you kind of know, as a veteran, where he's going to go. But then sometimes he'll mix it up, which is a good sign. And the way he throws the ball, it's just different coming off of his hand. When he lets it go, it's kind of like Cam Newton. You've seen Cam throw the ball? It's similar. A lot of power. He's also really good on his feet. He broke one in our first scrimmage and looked really good. Seeing him pull away and having that dual threat is hard to prepare for, like Lamar Jackson. That's why he's so good. He can do both. He's got that length, so once he gets started, it's hard to catch him. Trevor is just different, a different kind of guy.

Safety K'Von Wallace:

Just today, he threw from the opposing 30-yard line all the way to the 10-yard line. And he did it on the run. *It was amazing, I ain't going to lie. I didn't even think it was him. He was scrambling to his right, and he threw it off his hind legs. Just chunked it all the way to the 10-yard line. He threw it like 60, 70 yards. I remember another one he threw earlier in spring practice. He was falling down and getting tackled, but he just flicked it and it went 50 yards. I don't think the receiver caught it, but he still chucked it deep and almost had a big play. He has a cannon for an arm, and he's very accurate and tall. He's going to be great one day. You could tell early that he was talented and that he's been doing it for a long time. He's a natural-born quarterback. I consider him a lanky guy, but once he gets in that weight room and gets built—he's already smart and making good decisions. He can fit those tight throws. We see it all the time. We noticed when he came in that he was going to be a good player, but now just seeing him it's like, "Wow. This guy is going to be special." And he can run, too. He caught me one time in a scrimmage. He fumbled the ball and picked the fumble up, then he shook me and almost scored. So I underestimated his running ability. He's definitely a very good runner as well. People may think he's not going to be able to run, but he's going to surprise with his speed and his quickness.*

Running back Travis Etienne:

Probably when he's rolling outside of the pocket and he looks and just tosses it effortlessly and makes the throw. He has a couple of those every day that make you say "Wow." He's making throws on the run and throwing it like 50 yards. Everyone is just amazed, because it doesn't even look like he's trying. He took off running one practice and ran away from people. That's what really surprises me about him is seeing him take off like that. I honestly didn't think he was fast. So to see him take off like that and maintain his speed throughout the play is amazing. He has some plays where he has a freshman mistake, just because you don't know. But overall I feel like he's really developed for a freshman.

Linebacker Isaiah Simmons:

I think we were in a scrimmage. He rolled out to his right and on the run threw a bullet through like three people. It hit the receiver right in the hands, but the receiver dropped it. And Trevor was falling down. That's when we were like, "Whoa." He makes a lot of really crazy throws. It's mainly when he's scrambling. He's got a really, really strong arm. He overthrows a lot of people because his arm is so strong. He just throws the ball with so much ease, because he's really long. When he first got here, I heard he was good with his arm and his feet, so I kind of expected that. I wouldn't say he's as good on his feet as Kelly Bryant is, but he is really good on his feet.

Elliott:

The one that stands out to me was a roll-out to the left. He stays on the run, comes back across his body and hits the receiver down the field. We thought he was throwing the ball away, but somehow he found him. It was a good little distance, probably at least 35 or 40 yards. It was a lot like the throw he had in high school, running to his left. Very reminiscent of that one. He throws the ball very, very well on the run. And you expect that, because I saw that in high school. I saw him practice and play. But what has really caught my attention in the spring has been his presence in the pocket.

Typically, coaches elect to douse the flames of expectation surrounding a freshman even if he's worthy of the hype. Swinney and his staff took no such measures when asked about Lawrence during the spring. They were still couching this as a legitimate four-man battle between Bryant, Johnson, Lawrence and redshirt freshman Chase Brice. But it wasn't hard to read between the lines when Scott was asked if Lawrence was on the same level as Watson at the same point of his career.

"Yes," came the answer. "He's picking up things very quickly. He doesn't look like a true freshman who showed up in January. He's one of those guys who as soon as he learns it one time he knows it and can regurgitate it, and is doing really good in meetings....It's one thing knowing what side of the field to go to. That's the first thing, once the ball is snapped, is figuring out based on the safety structure am I working the field concept or am I working the boundary concept? Some of those times when he's trying to fit that ball in there it's not a situation where he's working the boundary and should have worked the field. It's where he knows he's in the boundary but he thinks he can make that throw. And obviously the speed is a little bit different at the college level. And again, we're not going to have to wait until the fall to be able to go against a fast secondary or linebacker group. We get to see it right here. So that's a huge benefit that we have. But he's definitely tested some throws, and he's made some too. So it's been fun to watch."

Everyone would get a chance to see for themselves in the spring game, a typically meaningless affair that was full of gravity and anticipation this time. From the moment he dropped back and unleashed a gorgeous deep-ball touchdown to Higgins early in the game, everything seemed different. The fans were ga-ga over Lawrence and the possibility that he might do for Clemson exactly what Tagovailoa did for Alabama three months earlier. A month later, Johnson would announce plans to transfer (he later ended up at Northwestern). And speculation swirled that Bryant, who had a miserable spring game, might be considering the same thing.

It was game on at quarterback for August and beyond. Lawrence was going to be hard to keep down for long.

CHAPTER 3

TEXAS HOLD 'EM

The quarterback battle was the biggest story of Clemson's preseason camp; nothing else was even close. High-profile competitions at this position were also the story of college football, with the Tigers joined by Alabama (Tua Tagovailoa versus Jalen Hurts), Georgia (Jake Fromm versus Justin Fields) and Ohio State (Dwayne Haskins versus Tate Martell). Tagovailoa's unforgettable performance in the CFP title game seemed to raise the stakes and the urgency with similar situations elsewhere, as it was assumed Alabama's offense was now going to be lethal and pyrotechnic after two years of a more plodding style with Hurts at the controls.

Four years earlier, offensive coordinator Chad Morris created a July splash when he told the media that freshman Deshaun Watson was going to play in that season's opener at Georgia. That set the tone for Watson's ascent to the starting role as a freshman, and now reporters were clamoring for some similar insight from the coaches about how they would handle Kelly Bryant and Trevor Lawrence. The big news entering camp was that the staff was totally open to playing two quarterbacks and had actually studied previous examples where it had worked elsewhere. Coaches reminded reporters that redshirt freshman Chase Brice was in the competition also.

An opening visit from Furman was viewed as a valuable examination with fans in the stands against an overmatched opponent. But the coaches had to sort it out fast in time for a trip to Texas A&M in the second game.

"The plan is to go into that first game with a plan of, 'OK, here's how everybody is going to play and how much they're going to play,' at least initially," quarterbacks coach Brandon Streeter said in July. "The plan is for at least those first three guys, they're going to play. How much? That's going to be determined by preseason camp and their performances in scrimmages during preseason, and then obviously the performance in especially the first game and first couple of games. But they're all going to play. Kelly is the guy right now. Make no mistake about it. He earned it. He is the guy who is going to go out there first, especially at the beginning of preseason camp. He has improved every single semester that he's been here. And he's earned that right. And obviously we have talented guys that are right there with him too that are going to have an opportunity....I know what Kelly does is that every time his back is against the wall, every time that he has pressure on him, he finds a way to shine. Especially in a competitive situation like we were last year. He's always improved, and that's what I've asked for."

The prospect of throwing a first-year quarterback into the din of A&M's Kyle Field is harrowing in most situations. It was reasonable to wonder how Lawrence would handle playing in front of 102,000 fans in his second game of college experience. Streeter, though, had no such concerns heading into August camp.

"He's built for that. He has a unique ability to have so much poise. It's similar to Deshaun: the pressure really doesn't bother him. So I would be shocked if it really bothered him in those bigger situations. By no means is any freshman going to go out there and be perfect, but he's the type of kid that can shrug it off and move on and be very successful. "

Another key element to the quarterback theme was how the head coach typically handles competition between a veteran trying to fight off a younger player. After Lawrence lit up the spring game and Bryant struggled mightily, it was assumed by many that Lawrence was going to take the job in camp and begin the season as the starter. Swinney, though, had proven before that he gives the benefit of the doubt to the veteran. Many coaches would have started Watson from the first game in 2014, because he was better than Cole Stoudt. But the battle had to play out on the field, and Watson had to make a decisive case. That year, the decisive case came in the third game at Florida State when Watson came in for Stoudt and put forth a superb performance in an overtime defeat. It was safe to assume the same philosophy would be used in this case, with Bryant beginning the season as the starter and the competition unfolding in game action. And Lawrence didn't merely have to be better than Bryant. He had to be unquestionably better, leaving no doubt.

"That's the way it's been always," Swinney told ESPN in July. "When you go back and look, I have started a lot of freshmen. Mitch Hyatt started as a true freshman. I've started a lot of redshirt freshmen. I've started a lot of true freshmen. Sammy Watkins came in and won the job on like the third day on campus. But it wasn't close. So that's just the way it is, but you have to earn it. The recruiting ranking is not how you earn it. You earn it through your effort, your accountability, doing what's right, embracing the concept of team and family and performance out on the field. You can't hide on that practice field. You either can or you can't. It becomes very obvious."

The quarterback competition overshadowed everything else, and for good reason: a lack of a consistent downfield passing game is what sealed Clemson's demise in the Sugar Bowl against Alabama. But Bryant wasn't the only reason for that deficiency in 2017; the drop-off at receiver after the loss of Mike Williams, Jordan Leggett and Artavis Scott was also a significant factor. The vanquishing of Alabama in Tampa, and the succession of victories in close games preceding it, was defined not just by exquisite throws from Watson but also game-changing catches above or around defensive backs within a close proximity. These leaping, stretching catches through contact were not present with much consistency in 2017. And it caught up with the offense in New Orleans, where Deon Cain had three crucial drops in pivotal situations. The coaches were confident that this would change, and in a hurry. Tee Higgins was ready to blossom as a sophomore after he gained comfort and confidence late in his freshman season. Unlike Cain, Higgins had the six-foot-four height and long arms to go up and get balls in his vicinity. On the other side, Amari Rodgers was viewed as an upgrade from Ray-Ray McCloud. Hunter Renfrow was always a tough cover. And the coaches were singing the praises of senior backup Trevion Thompson.

But it doesn't end there. Not when you've cultivated a distinction as Wide Receiver U. Clemson stockpiles receivers like it stockpiles defensive linemen, coming at you in dizzying and demoralizing waves. And the next wave came in the form of Justyn Ross, whom Jeff Scott and Todd Bates managed to pull out of the state of Alabama. Ross was the top prospect in the state, and it's darned near impossible for anyone other than Alabama or Auburn to come in and grab the No. 1 player. The last school to do it before Clemson did in February 2018: Florida State's nabbing of Jameis Winston in 2012. That explains the unrestrained, fist-pumping joy shown by Scott and Swinney on National Signing Day when Ross followed through and made his pledge official. Ross did not enroll in January, so it didn't seem like a lock that he'd come in over the summer and make an immediate splash. But right away, he showed an advanced mental foundation to go with the six-foot-four frame, the freaky athleticism, the staggering leaping ability and those big, sticky hands that plucked the ball out of the air.

"He's got a really good foundation," Swinney said at the time. "He's just naturally strong. He does some things instinctively that are hard to coach. So that's really fun to be able to have a guy like that. He's got a bright future, and he loves it. Loves to be coached. Great effort guy."

Another freshman, Derion Kendrick, created optimism that the Tigers would be much more formidable on the outside. The coaches were supremely confident that Clemson's downfield passing game would be better in 2018 regardless of who was throwing the passes.

"We're much better at wideout than we were at this time last year," Swinney said. "It ain't even close. There was a lot of coaching going on last year at that position.…We're night and day at wideout from where we were this time last year. Just knowledge, details, understanding."

The quarterback battle raged through camp, and on Monday of Furman week, Swinney named Bryant the starter. Bryant showed significant improvement in his downfield passing during camp, and that was a big factor in his edging of Lawrence for the job. But while announcements of the starting quarterback often bring closure, this felt like just the beginning. Lawrence was going to play early and often as the staff rotated quarterbacks. And the staff seemed to have zero problem doing the two-quarterback thing as long as it took—mainly because they believed the offense was going to be just fine regardless of who was running the show. What they saw in a 48–7 romp over Furman did little to change their thinking. Bryant threw for 132 yards and a touchdown on aN 11-of-17 clip while rushing for 44 yards on 5 carries. Lawrence threw for 137 yards and 3 touchdowns while completing 9 of 15 throws and rushing for a yard on 3 attempts. "I didn't see anything from today that said we're only going to play one quarterback next week," said Scott, the co-offensive coordinator. The head coach: "I didn't see anything that would say, 'This guy doesn't deserve to play.'"

Bryant was shaky early and gave way to Lawrence, who had a few sputters of his own before finding his groove and giving the offense a spark. Though it did seem the offense looked different with the freshman spreading the ball around and firing lasers with effortless flicks of his wrist, it was also true that Bryant gave the Tigers a necessary running dimension.

"Both had some mistakes and both missed a couple of easy throws," Swinney said. "But I think that was just kind of the emotion and adrenaline of the first game. But they both settled in and made some big-time plays.…

You see what Trevor can do. He's a special talent, and he's just going to get better."

Ross had a 15-yard touchdown catch in the third quarter, but the jitters were obvious. Swinney noticed that Ross's leg was shaking on his first play. "It's just so funny. It doesn't matter how talented they are, how much success they've had. It's just a different deal. You cannot simulate game day."

You also cannot simulate the aura of a bloodthirsty, primetime crowd at Texas A&M. This was the real test for Clemson's new two-quarterback experiment, for Lawrence and those young receivers. The presence of Jimbo Fisher in College Station also provided an interesting twist to a matchup that was scheduled years before, when everything was still hunky-dory with Fisher at Florida State.

In recent years, Swinney has played a role in chasing established, respected coaches from their posts. Surely Clemson's ascent to the top of the mountain in 2015 contributed to Steve Spurrier hanging up his visor at South Carolina in the middle of that season. Frank Beamer once lorded over the ACC at Virginia Tech, but two whippings at the hands of Clemson in 2011 (including one for the conference championship) and another in 2012 showed him it was going to be hard to get back to the top. (He retired in 2015.) Oklahoma's Bob Stoops, who abruptly retired in the summer of 2017, just couldn't get the Sooners back to the same exalted level. Clemson stood in the way in 2015, destroying Oklahoma in the CFP semifinal. A year earlier, a 40–6 bludgeoning at the hands of Clemson in the Russell Athletic Bowl caused Stoops to purge his offensive staff. Urban Meyer won a national title in 2014, but the only time his Buckeyes returned to the playoff over the next four seasons they were blown to bits by Clemson in the 2016 semifinal. (He retired after the 2018 season.) Bobby Petrino came agonizingly close to beating Clemson three times but finished 0-5 against Swinney, who would give him a 77–16 parting gift in November 2018—eight days before Louisville fired him. Once upon a time, Paul Johnson had bragging rights over Clemson and frustrated Tigers fans to no end while winning four of his first five against Swinney. But Johnson lost six of his last seven against Clemson, all in resounding fashion, before leaving Tech in December 2018.

Swinney alone didn't chase Fisher from Tallahassee, but it would be hard to argue that Clemson's vast success didn't play a role. In addition to the Tigers becoming the ACC's supreme being from 2015 to 2017, after the Seminoles ruled the ACC for the previous three years and won the national title in 2013, Clemson had created great distance between the two in the areas of facilities, overall infrastructure, branding and coaching continuity.

This was surely a sore spot for Fisher as he battled with his administration to devote more to the arms race against the monster Swinney had created. Texas A&M had no such problem forking out the cash, and Fisher's departure from Florida State felt more like a divorce.

As the visit to College Station loomed, Clemson fans were initially more preoccupied with what was going on at Alabama. The Crimson Tide had played their opener in Orlando against Louisville in what was billed by some as an intersectional showdown. Tagovailoa and the Crimson Tide's offense made a mockery of that in destroying the Cardinals 51–14. Swinney's first goal in the team meeting room reads: "Win the opener." For some fans in 2018, a variation seemed to rule: "Win the opener…and then fret over what Alabama did in the opener." This was an irresistible topic given that Clemson possessed a young quarterback who had the tools and the weapons to facilitate a similar offensive onslaught. Some scoreboard watching and benchmarking was also natural given that Clemson and Alabama had met in the playoff three years in a row. But while people on the outside were focused on one team from the SEC West, the people inside the football offices had to put their full attention on another group from the same division: the Texas A&M team that was next on the schedule.

The Tigers traveled to the Lone Star State with style and swagger. The day before the game, Austin Bryant and Christian Wilkins descended the stairs of the charter flight wearing cowboy hats. The Tigers made big statements in 2017 in primetime games at Louisville, Virginia Tech and South Carolina. The plan here was to do the same, to leave no doubt.

Clemson's defensive staff entered the game concerned about how Fisher, a skilled tactician, was going to attack them. They had just one game of film to go on. Like Clemson, A&M had been rotating quarterbacks. Fisher had hired Darrell Dickey from Memphis to be his offensive coordinator, and Dickey's style was different from what Fisher ran in Tallahassee. On top of that, Fisher had hired Mike Elko as defensive coordinator. Elko was a respected name who had been at Notre Dame and Wake Forest, and there was some doubt there as well as to how he would defend Clemson.

After sixteen minutes on a rain-soaked field, the Tigers were feeling plenty comfortable. Kelly Bryant led a touchdown drive of 75 yards on seven plays. Then, Lawrence was inserted and an instant bolt of lightning: a lofted pass to Tee Higgins near the sideline, followed by Higgins leaping high over a defensive back, followed by Higgins taking off and outrunning everyone else to the end zone. A 64-yard touchdown strike, and the first signal of just how deadly this offense could be. But the Tigers couldn't administer the

Kelly Bryant runs for a touchdown in the first quarter against Texas A&M.

knockout punch. They were close late in the first half, facing fourth-and-goal at the A&M 1-yard line. A touchdown meant a 21–6 lead and a deflated crowd with less than two minutes left. Bryant fumbled the snap from Justin Falcinelli, and the drive ended.

Clemson did go up 21–6 with five minutes left in the third quarter, but things almost got out of hand from there. The Aggies sliced up the back end of the Tigers' defense, finding open spaces and making some exceptional competitive plays. Down 28–20 late, A&M moved right down the field and was in position to score when Quartney Davis got loose over the middle and raced for the left pylon. K'Von Wallace stayed after it and gave chase, diving and reaching to punch the ball from Davis's grasp as Davis lunged for the pylon. The ball sailed past the pylon and was ruled a touchback. Fisher was furious that it wasn't ruled out of bounds at the 1-yard line instead.

The offense couldn't get a first down after taking over with 2:13 left. A&M got the ball back and reached the end zone when Kellen Mond found Kendrick Rogers for a 24-yard touchdown. Actually, Mond's pass found the hands of Wallace, but he couldn't bring it in. Wallace deflected the ball, and it bounced right into the hands of Rogers, who corralled it while falling to the ground. The Aggies needed a 2-point conversion to tie the game with

Tee Higgins goes high for a throw from Trevor Lawrence before turning and heading for the end zone.

46 seconds left, but Christian Wilkins bulled into the backfield and drew a holding penalty to end that threat. Hunter Renfrow grabbed the onside kick to end the game.

The operative sound from Clemson's fans was less cheer and more a heaving sigh of relief. A&M had amassed 25 first downs to 14 for the Tigers, out-gained Clemson 501–413 and thrown for 430 yards.

"We had opportunities to take control of the game in the first half, and we didn't take advantage of it," Swinney said afterward.

Bryant gave the offense what it needed in the second half, providing a calming influence that Lawrence probably was not ready to offer at that point. Bryant used his arm and his legs and his veteran presence on two crucial touchdown drives in the second half.

"We want to continue to get Trevor in the game," Swinney said. "He's a special talent. We've seen that. But you've just got to love what you've seen out of Kelly....I think both guys can help our football team."

Brent Venables spent the offseason worried about his secondary, and Mond's sensational showing justified those concerns. The back end often looked lost, but the defensive line didn't do a good job of containing Mond either. The belief that Clemson would shut down everyone with its NFL

Dabo Swinney celebrates with Trevor Lawrence after Lawrence's connection with Tee Higgins for a long touchdown in the second quarter.

defensive line seemed a bit too fanciful as the orange-clad knot of fans filed into the streets of College Station.

"There's no question we've got to get better," Venables said afterward. "We got exposed at times."

As Swinney concluded his postgame press conference and stepped down from an elevated platform, he walked slowly. A crazy-train second half in the heart of Texas seemed to age him a few years.

"Man, I'm sore," he said. "I feel like I just played."

CHAPTER 4

HOME SWEET HOME

I n January 2017, a cluster of college coaches sat in a room at Jennings High School waiting to make their pitches to Travis Etienne; his mother, Donnetta; and coach Rusty Phelps. The assistants from LSU, Tennessee and Louisiana Tech brought big personalities into the room, telling jokes and stories and trying to connect in a way that most coaches connect. But there was another coach sitting there who didn't say much at all, didn't make small talk with the other guys, in large part because he was a long way from home and had no background or ties in Louisiana.

"We were taking the coaches into a conference room one by one and hearing them out," Donnetta said. "All these other men are—you know how men go— rah-rah-rah, talking man stuff and being loud or whatever. But Coach Tony is just there sitting and waiting quietly in a chair and not saying anything. He never said a word. He was courteous. He engaged when he was asked a question, but he was never boastful about what he was coming to do."

Coach Tony, of course, would be Tony Elliott. The same guy who, as Clemson's chief play-caller, had helped engineer a 35–31 victory over Alabama in the national title game just three days earlier. The day before that game in Tampa, Elliott and Dabo Swinney were stunned to see Fort Myers back Darrian Felix commit to Oregon. They tried to convince Felix to follow through with his scheduled visit to Clemson, but the deal was done. And now they were scrambling.

Elliott knew about Etienne, but only vaguely. He reached out to Phelps and asked the coach to tell him more about the kid as a person. Right away, he knew he had to go visit him as soon as possible. The triumph over the Crimson Tide, sealed with 21 fourth-quarter points against Alabama's crazy-good defense, was just hours old when Elliott called Etienne and asked him if he was interested in the Tigers. The answer: "Definitely, Coach."

The final day of the dead period was January 11, the day after Clemson returned from Tampa to that joyous, blissful scene with all the fans outside the west end zone of Death Valley—back when the Tigers' first national title since 1981 still didn't feel totally real. A day later, Elliott was on a flight to the small town of ten thousand in west Louisiana, seventy miles from the Texas border.

The other coaches already had built relationships with Etienne's inner circle. Elliott was starting from scratch. And fresh off a win on college football's biggest stage, he didn't want to create the appearance that he was full of himself.

"I show up, and it's a who's-who," Elliott recalled. "You've got LSU in the office already. Tennessee is in the office already. And I'm here walking in, had never met the coach and had never met the kid. I'd never met the coaches from LSU and Tennessee. I didn't want them thinking I was walking in thinking they had no shot. I was actually walking in thinking we might

LSU, Travis Etienne's home-state school, didn't express genuine interest in Etienne until it was too late.

not have a shot because we've never even met this kid. I just wanted to make sure I presented myself well, represented Coach Swinney well and presented what our program is all about. Because our program is not built off talk."

Elliott deferred to the other coaches, allowing them to have their private meetings first. Last in line, he knew Donnetta was exhausted by the process. But he connected by being open and honest about himself, his life and the Clemson community he was hoping Etienne would come visit. So Elliott stood out by not standing out, by doing away with the standard sales pitches and promises the family had heard plenty of. "I just really can't explain it," Donnetta said. "He didn't have an ego trip thing. He made us want to see what Clemson was all about."

Previously, Clemson wasn't even on Etienne's radar. He had visits lined up to Tennessee a day later (January 13), to Texas A&M on January 20 and to LSU on January 27. But things began to change when Elliott presented an offer in that conference room at the school. Donnetta says it was the thirty-fourth and final scholarship offer her son received. While students and school personnel mobbed LSU running backs coach Jabbar Juluke and posed for pictures with him, Elliott was quietly working some magic just by being himself. "Nobody really knew anything about Clemson," Donnetta said. "Nobody knew who this coach was."

Things are much different now in Jennings, with Etienne having established himself not just as one of the major figures at Clemson but one of the major faces of college football. He made an immediate splash as a freshman in 2017. And then he broke out and became a superstar in 2018. The powerful, explosive back has made orange a popular color in his hometown, located three hours from New Orleans.

Clemson is a recruiting machine, and evidence of that comes every year with the addition of elite players such as Trevor Lawrence, Xavier Thomas and K.J. Henry. Justyn Ross and Tee Higgins were the best of the best in high school, aggressively sought by everyone. Most of the time, when Clemson signs a player it's the fruition of years of relationship-building and trust. Etienne's story is so much different, built on last-minute improvisation. Even before Felix's surprise pledge to Oregon, Clemson's staff had parted ways with Cordarrian Richardson in December. In the summer of 2016, Clemson's staff told Philadelphia running back D'Andre Swift (now at Georgia) they didn't have room for him because of their commitment to Richardson.

So now, less than a month before National Signing Day, Elliott needed a running back. He had no relationship with California back Najee Harris, who would end up at Alabama. Same with Mississippi stud Cam Akers, who'd committed to Florida State in late December. Back in the summer of 2016, Etienne had reached out to Clemson via a coach in Louisiana who had a relationship with Tigers staffer Mickey Conn. Etienne was interested in Clemson, and the coach told Conn he was going to be special. But Elliott had to move on. "I told him if something changes we'll take a look at him," Elliott said. "But we had a commitment from Richardson, and there was nothing we could do. Because that's our policy."

Fast-forwarding to January 2017, the Etienne family was stirred by the visit from Elliott. This came after they ate nachos and watched Clemson and Alabama, Etienne telling his mom the Tigers had no shot "because mama, it's Bama," and his mom screaming, "I told you!" after Hunter Renfrow's touchdown catch with one second left. They thought about canceling the scheduled visit to Tennessee and going to Clemson to attend the Tigers' championship parade, but Donnetta said they followed through on their plans as a matter of courtesy to the Volunteers' staff. On that visit to Knoxville, Etienne was riding down an elevator with several other recruits. He told the group about his offer from Clemson. The response from one of the recruits, as relayed by Donnetta: "Why are you even here? If I had a Clemson offer, I wouldn't have come on this visit."

The day after they returned to Jennings from Knoxville, Elliott was back, and this time he brought Swinney for an in-home visit hosted by Etienne's grandmother. When Elliott and Swinney left the home that night, Etienne had cancelled his scheduled visit to Texas A&M the following weekend. The family was going to check out Clemson instead.

"Travis gave me a call and said, 'Dad, we're going to Clemson,'" said his father, Travis Etienne Sr. "I was like: 'Where did that come from, TJ? Clemson?' I hadn't heard nothing about Clemson. And all of a sudden, we're going to Clemson."

And that's where a gut feeling became a virtual certainty. The family was able to tour the glistening operations facility that the football program would move into soon thereafter. The small-town feel and the welcoming atmosphere made it feel like home to Etienne, even if he was 741 miles from home.

"We fell in love with Clemson," his mother said. "And I fell in love with the people. They were so warm and inviting, and they were like family. Travis is a sheltered kid. You wanted him to go somewhere where he felt like he was part of family. You can imagine coming in on the thirty-fourth scholarship offer, you've seen a lot of people and a lot of places. You're getting the royal

Travis Etienne was a backup in 2017 as a freshman but became the full-time starter as a sophomore.

treatment from everybody. But not everybody individualizes the experience for you. Coach Dabo, he gave us a hug. No other coaches did that. All the other coaches made it feel like you were joining a football team. But Dabo and Coach Tony made us feel like we were joining a family."

Before they left that Sunday, Etienne had his exit interview with Swinney in the coach's office at the stadium. Amid all the boxes that were being packed for the move across Perimeter Road, Etienne privately committed to Swinney. His father remembers Swinney tossing him an All-In chip on the way out. Clemson still had to fend off LSU. When the Etiennes returned to Jennings, a contingent from Baton Rouge was waiting: new head coach Ed Orgeron, Juluke and star offensive coordinator Matt Canada. On the outside, the Bayou Bengals were the presumed front-runner. Etienne grew up rooting for LSU and making regular ninety-minute trips to attend their home games. It wasn't hard to imagine him going to Texas A&M, where he'd committed before backing off the previous August. But Clemson? It seemed like a stretch.

Reality, though, was different. LSU under Les Miles was lukewarm toward Etienne, putting all its focus on Akers. By the time Akers announced for Florida State, Miles was gone and Orgeron was going hard after Etienne.

But it was too late. "LSU was late. Period," Donnetta said. "They were late. They showed us no love. Let's be honest. They showed us no love."

The visit from the LSU entourage did little to change Etienne's thought process. He'd already made up his mind he wasn't going to go to Baton Rouge for his scheduled visit the next weekend. Instead of waiting until signing day, he decided to make the announcement on his birthday. So on January 26, four days after he returned from Clemson and one day before he was supposed to visit LSU, he had a ceremony at his school and announced he was going to "the real Death Valley." LSU fans, across the state and even in Etienne's hometown, exploded in anger. All sorts of nastiness gushed forth on social media, to the point that Etienne's father had to delete the Facebook app from his phone.

"I got friends who are still mad at me about that, 'the real Death Valley,'" Travis Sr. said. "I'm like, 'Why you picking on my child? You're not the one going to school.' Everybody here has changed their tune now. A bunch of them are Clemson fans now."

It's been quite the conversion for a small town in the heart of Cajun Country. And it all started that day in the office of the high school, when there was something about this unassuming coach from Clemson that Etienne and his mother just couldn't shake.

Elliott:

> *I just wanted to get in the room, get one-on-one, and say this is who I am, this is why I'm here and hopefully you guys have enough interest to at least come check us out and see. I think she* [Donnetta] *appreciated the transparency of how honest I was with our process, as opposed to going the recruiting route. I think they had done enough of the recruiting. They were tired of that.*

CHAPTER 5

TREVOR, THEN TURMOIL

Late on the afternoon of September 22 in Atlanta, assorted coaches and players were almost finished with their postgame media obligations following a 49–21 spanking of Georgia Tech. These interviews were taking place in the Yellow Jackets' weight room, which was somewhat fitting because the Tigers had once again shown how much bigger, stronger and faster they were than the program that used to give Clemson fits early in Dabo Swinney's head-coaching tenure.

Jeff Scott, the Tigers' fourth-year co–offensive coordinator, was in a great mood as he reflected on what he'd just seen from Trevor Lawrence. The freshman from nearby Cartersville had just put on a homecoming show in the Tigers' fourth game, making an emphatic statement that it was his time to be the starting quarterback after four weeks of a rotation predicated on Kelly Bryant starting. Scott had answered the last question and was headed back to the locker room. This writer stopped him and reminded him of something he'd said back in August when the world wanted to know how the staff would handle juggling two quarterbacks:

"Coach Swinney says all the time he doesn't mind playing a freshman or sophomore. But if it's against a senior, a guy with experience, it's got to be a knockout shot." Those were Scott's words during August camp. Scott was asked if Lawrence's tapestry on this day—13 for 18 passing, 176 yards, four touchdowns—constituted a knockout punch in the quarterback battle. Scott elected not to comment, but the smile on his face said it all: Clemson had found its quarterback, and Lawrence was everything the staff thought he was when they signed him.

Tre Lamar forces an early fumble at Georgia Tech that is recovered by Clelin Ferrell for a touchdown.

The fact that Bryant held on to his starting job into the fourth game of the season made this competition sound complicated. Fact is, it never was. Swinney and his staff needed to see something definitive to elevate Lawrence to the starting role, and he showed them exactly that at Georgia Tech. He was in on six possessions. Clemson scored touchdowns on five of them, including a late exclamation-point 30-yard strike to Tee Higgins after Swinney put the front-line guys back in "to finish the right way." The offense mustered one first down and no points on Bryant's two first-half possessions, and Bryant came in on mop-up duty to lead the offense on a touchdown drive. "We're going to enjoy tonight, that's what we're going to do," Swinney told reporters. "We're not going to set depth charts here in the postgame press conference." On the bus ride back to Clemson that night, Swinney decided it was time to make the change.

Numerous voices on the outside said it was time to make Lawrence the starter, including this observer in a day-after column for Tigerillustrated.com:

> *We've called it like we've seen it the whole time. We said exiting spring practice that Lawrence was capable of starting the entire season and would be hard to hold off for long. We also said Bryant was, in fact, capable of improving on his first season as the starter.*

Bryant did improve, and that's a great credit to him. But No. 16 is just a different type of player who makes the offense look different when he's on the field. As much as everyone on the outside wanted this drama to follow a set script, the reality was it was going to unfold organically. Resolution to the competition was going to be one of those "you'll know it when you see it" type of deals.

Some folks wanted so bad for Lawrence to be the guy RIGHT NOW that they saw that moment in the spring game, or last week against Georgia Southern. For those who are detached from the extremes of tribal affiliation, that moment came yesterday. It was the right call to start Bryant the first four games. Now it's the right call to start Lawrence.

On Monday, five days before a visit from Syracuse, Swinney made it official by listing Lawrence as the starter on the weekly depth chart. It was big news but not controversial news. Quarterbacks coach Brandon Streeter informed Bryant of the change Sunday night. Privately, Swinney told the team the next morning and presented stats to back up the move. Bryant: 36 of 54 passing for 461 yards, 66.7 percent completions, two touchdowns, one interception, 8.5 yards per attempt, 146.9 rating, 130 yards rushing. Lawrence: 39 of 60 passing for 600 yards, 65 percent completions, nine touchdowns, two interceptions, 10 yards per attempt, 191.8 rating, 24 yards rushing. Bryant had been in for twenty possessions, and the offense has scored seven touchdowns on those drives. Lawrence had been in for twenty-four possessions, and the offense has scored thirteen touchdowns on those drives. Points per possession with Bryant in the game: 2.6. Points per possession with Lawrence in the game: 4.04.

As much as Bryant and Lawrence and everyone had cast their relationship and their handling of the two-quarterback system in a positive light, in truth it was a difficult and awkward situation. Bryant felt like he'd done nothing to lose the job, and on top of that, his body language often looked less than enthused when he stood on the sideline and watched Lawrence. The freshman was confident in his abilities also, confident that he was the better guy. It was true that both of them genuinely liked the other. But it was also true that they were both supreme competitors at the highest level of college football. "It was just a weird situation," Lawrence later recalled. "He's an older guy who has built relationships with these guys for four years and a great dude. That was more uncomfortable than anything on the field this year."

The next morning, a few hours before Swinney's normal Tuesday press conference, this writer received a tip that Bryant had not been at practice the night before. We reached out to football communications director Ross Taylor, who could not confirm it. Taylor briefed Swinney on the tip, and at his press conference, the coach voluntarily broke the news that he had given Bryant the previous day off. The coach also shared that it was an extremely difficult conversation with Bryant, who'd amassed a 16-2 record as the starting quarterback.

"It's a bad day to be the head coach. Most days it's good. But it's a bad day. Because I love Kelly. It was emotional. Emotional for him. Tough day.... It's tough, tough. Because he's played well. And there's not a guy that's ever been here as long as I've been at Clemson, there's not a guy that's been as committed to this program as Kelly Bryant. There's not a better leader. This guy is the epitome of what you want. He's what you want your son to be like. I love him. Like a son. So it was a very difficult conversation. And he's very disappointed. But I don't have any doubt that he'll show up and go back to work and respond."

The NCAA's more relaxed redshirt rules allow a graduate player to transfer, preserve a year of eligibility and play right away the next year provided that player sees action in four or fewer games. Bryant had played in four games in 2018. Swinney was asked at the press conference if Bryant had conveyed an interest in transferring.

"No. No. No. We just talked about a lot of things. But I don't have any doubt he'll be right here and ready to go and get back on the horse and ride....If I was worried about [a transfer], or if I was deceitful in some way or something like that, I could've huddled the coaches up and said, 'Hey, let's make sure we start [Bryant] for Syracuse and that way he's got no option.' But that's not how I operate. I don't think like that. I don't operate that way. I mean, I'm just trying to do what's right. And I'm not ever going to apologize for that."

About six hours later, the story became a full-blown controversy. Bryant showed up and went through the normal Tuesday meetings. But then when practice began, he was nowhere to be found. Soon thereafter, Matt Connolly of *The State* newspaper reported that Bryant was a no-show for the second day in a row. On top of all this, it was Bryant's twenty-second birthday. The last sight of him, according to a source with the team, was when he was walking out of the football facility to the parking lot with belongings from his locker and a birthday cake. On the other side of the monstrous Allen N. Reeves football complex, the Tigers were going through practice while one of their key figures was going out the door for good. Swinney sent some staffers in search of Bryant, but he was gone. The last thing Swinney had told Bryant earlier in the day was that he needed an answer by 10:50 a.m. Wednesday morning, his normal time on an ACC media teleconference. When Swinney returned to his office after practice, he had a text from Bryant saying he was leaving.

The next morning came another gut punch. In normal transfer situations, the player and the coach come up with prepared statements and the school announces the news. In this case, Bryant gave the scoop to *Greenville News* reporter Manie Robinson. In the article, Bryant was quoted as saying his demotion was "a slap in the face" and he wasn't treated fairly. Soon thereafter, Swinney was on the ACC teleconference and was asked about Bryant's comments. "Nothing changes how I feel about him. I think he's one of the best young people I've ever been around. It's impossible for me to say anything bad about him. And I hope nobody else does either. Just wish him well. Support him even though you might not like his decision, and we've got to move on."

Swinney makes himself available to the media after every Wednesday practice during the season, and normally this event is attended by eight to ten people. But on this evening, media attendance was closer to fifty with cameras all around and Swinney being asked to comment yet again on Bryant's departure. A few former players, including members of the 2016 team that won the national title, popped off on Twitter and ridiculed Swinney for promoting Lawrence. Meanwhile, Clemson was trying to pull together and prepare to face the team that handed the Tigers their only regular-season loss of 2017 after Bryant left the game with a concussion.

An excerpt from a column by this writer that week on Tigerillustrated.com:

> For months, Dabo Swinney has publicly wondered why people are so dang interested in a quarterback competition. He has said it's no different than competition at any other position. Just last night, he noted that the media didn't flock to practice asking about Sean Pollard after Cade Stewart started over Pollard at right guard against Texas A&M.
>
> Quarterback is treated differently because it is different. How many times have you heard a coach say "My right guard is 27-2 as a starter?" How often have you heard a coach say he gave his demoted defensive tackle a day off from practice to cope with it? How many times has a coach appeared genuinely distraught over a depth-chart shakeup at receiver?
>
> Swinney's take on this is not a big deal. Coaches talk to their team through the media all the time, and our guess is that's the basis for his "it's no different than any other position" position. On matters that are

a big deal relating to recent developments at quarterback, from this corner Swinney has handled it flawlessly. Which is to say that, in the course of making a difficult but justified decision to promote Trevor Lawrence, he has done everything possible to honor the feelings, the point of view, the reputation and the legacy of the player he demoted....

We've been around him since 2004, and even when he was a receivers coach he was relentlessly building up his players. Lavishing them with praise that in some cases might not have been deserved. From then to now, if you ask him about a third-string bust he's probably going to tell you that the guy is this close to breaking out. Even he has gone on record saying it's on the coaches when they miss on a prospect, that it's not the player's fault. It's all on them.

The former walk-on always has a soft spot not just for the stars who have made him a very rich man, but also for the obscure guys who are busting it and will probably never do much of note. Swinney's elaborate touting of his players is something people like to joke about in some instances. But in this instance, it is a boldface confirmation that the man loves his players and almost always gives them the benefit of the doubt. And now some of his former players are going after him for a decision that is 100-percent defensible. Shameful.

There have been some slaps in the face over the past few days, no doubt. Except they're not coming from the head coach. He's had their backs a lot more lately than they've had his.

This team was not merely trying to move on from a transaction. It was much closer to the team grieving the loss of a loved one. Some players weren't happy Bryant chose to bail on the team during the season, and some didn't like his choice of words in describing Swinney's decision. But Bryant was still a beloved figure on the team, an integral part of its fabric even before he became the starter in 2017. And now he was gone.

"It's sad to see," Brent Venables said. "I just hate it, just the big picture. I'm just a loyal guy. I believe in just fighting and sticking to it. That's just me. That's easy to say. I'm not sitting here trying to judge. He had such an incredible legacy here with his leadership and his toughness and his accomplishments: 'I just keep fighting and control what I can control.' And, 'My teammates are here and this is my team,' that's how we all looked at him. I've probably said too much. I've got my own problems. But as a member of this team and as a coach, I've always—and I still do—hold Kelly in very high regard because I know the pressure that goes with that is different than

Dabo Swinney exits the bus before the Syracuse game after one of the longest, most difficult weeks of his coaching career.

there is at middle linebacker. I know that. I just don't think that if there's opportunities down the road that you have to look somewhere else, because there's those same opportunities right here. But that's just me."

Less than six months earlier, an ESPN crew came to Clemson to broadcast the spring game, and the major topic was the Tigers' stocked quarterback cupboard. Former five-star signee Hunter Johnson left a month later. And now Bryant's departure made Chase Brice the no. 2 guy. Taking reps at the third-string quarterback spot during Syracuse week: none other than Hunter Renfrow. Bryant would later end up at Missouri.

The day before the Syracuse game, Streeter traveled to Greenville for a previously scheduled speaking engagement at a downtown restaurant. The Bryant situation was the elephant in the room as hundreds of Clemson fans gathered to eat lunch and hear some inside scoop about the situation. Streeter went down his list of talking points and finally got to Bryant. He became choked up for a moment before gathering himself and concluding the speech.

On game day, Clemson had the look of a team that had been through a week of monumental distractions. Lawrence didn't look totally comfortable in his first start, losing a fumble on the offense's second play. Syracuse was moving the ball consistently on the Tigers' vaunted defense. But then came the sum of all fears at the 4:56 mark of the second quarter: Lawrence sprawled on the turf and being attended to by trainers after diving for extra yardage and absorbing a helmet to the neck and shoulder area. It looked like a concussion, and it could have been worse given the severity of the hit. This was exactly the scenario Swinney presented to Bryant after the demotion: Lawrence could get hurt, and you could be the starter again. Lawrence could not play well, and you could be the starter again. The staff had stressed to Bryant that it was still an open competition, that Bryant could still play his way back into the starting job just as Lawrence did. But there the team stood in the locker room at halftime, down 16–7 and minus Bryant and Lawrence. Everyone looked at Brice, the redshirt freshman who'd cultivated a reputation in practice as a lovable gunslinger—a gamer who was going to help them do big things one day. It's just that everyone thought that day would come in 2020 or 2021, not the fifth game of 2018.

The prevailing feeling inside Death Valley was gloom and doom. Fans were in a panic over Lawrence's injury and in a rage over Bryant's departure. Star corner Trayvon Mullen sprained his ankle in the second quarter and was out. It felt like players were dropping like flies. In the press box, writers joked about going to the Music City Bowl instead of back to the College

Trevor Lawrence against Syracuse in his first collegiate start. He was injured in the second quarter while diving for extra yardage.

Football Playoff. There was a feeling, and not an unreasonable one, that the Tigers were on the verge of being blown out of their own stadium by Syracuse. The visitors had 221 yards in the first 30 minutes, but three times the defense held the Orange to field goals after their offense had first downs inside Clemson's 31-yard line.

On the second drive of the third quarter, Brice threw an interception to give Syracuse the ball in Clemson territory. Over the headsets, Swinney told his offensive staff they were going to have to lean on the run to help take the pressure off Brice. Even if Syracuse stacked the line of scrimmage to take away the run and make Brice beat them with his arm, the Tigers were going to be stubborn and try to win it the old-fashioned way. The Orange was 38 yards away from making it a 23–7 game. But the defense held, and Syracuse couldn't even get in field-goal range.

A circus catch by Renfrow from Brice down the seam converted a third down and gained 28 yards to set up a field goal that made it 16–10. Things seemed somewhat manageable now. And then, on second down for Syracuse, A.J. Terrell stepped in front of an Eric Dungey pass and picked it off. This supplied a major jolt of hope and emotion as Terrell returned the interception 20 yards to set up another field goal that made the score 16–13. It felt like Clemson was going to be OK.

Syracuse moved the ball to midfield, but Clemson produced another stop and a punt. Everything was in the Tigers' favor as the ball sailed toward return man Amari Rodgers, who'd fumbled a punt earlier but recovered it. He lost this one too and didn't get it back. Syracuse recovered at the Clemson 10 and then cashed in with a touchdown. The Tigers were down 23–13, and the foreboding feeling was back inside the stadium. Syracuse was on the verge of handing this powerhouse another stunning defeat.

But the offense responded, and Brice provided the spark with back-to-back passes to Justyn Ross for 16 and 15 yards. Then Travis Etienne took over with a 17-yard burst to the Syracuse 26, then a 26-yard dash to the end zone to trim the margin to 23–20. Clemson forced a punt but couldn't move the ball. Then the defense forced another punt that put the Tigers deep in their territory with 6:06 left. A holding penalty on Clemson was tacked on, placing the ball at the 6-yard line.

The Tigers pounded the run to get to midfield, giving the ball to the backs seven straight times against Syracuse's gassed defense. Etienne ran for 2 yards on third-and-3 from the Syracuse 49, and there was no doubt Clemson was going for fourth-and-1 with 2:50 on the clock. But then backup right guard Gage Cervenka committed a false-start penalty in his haste to pull to the left side on a lead block for Etienne. Now it was fourth-and-6 from the Clemson 48. "Everything that could have gone wrong went wrong," said center Justin Falcinelli.

Swinney had already used a timeout to set up the play that was derailed by Cervenka's penalty. He swallowed hard and kept his offense on the field, leaving it in the hands of Brice when the better decision seemed to be punting and relying on the defense to get the ball back. "I think you punt the football here," ESPN analyst Todd Blackledge told viewers.

Swinney and his coaches had been saying all along that they could win with Brice, and then Brice delivered by threading a perfect throw to Higgins near the Clemson sideline. Syracuse was in a zone defense, which meant that Higgins was to find a soft spot on a circle route that started inside and then wound its way back to the sideline. That part was easy. But getting the ball to him with three defenders in the vicinity was another matter. Brice's pass had the perfect velocity and accuracy needed to hit Higgins for a 20-yard gain. "The game is on the line and he throws a strike," Swinney said. "Just unbelievable moxie."

On the next play, Brice pulled the ball and ran it himself after the defensive end aggressively pursued the running back. Brice found open grass and reached the 20 before lowering his shoulder and dragging a cluster of

Travis Etienne celebrates a touchdown against Syracuse.

Backup Chase Brice keeps for a big run on the Tigers' go-ahead touchdown drive against Syracuse.

Syracuse defenders all the way to the 15. Bryant's spirit was still very much present on this day, as everyone was still trying to process the fact that he was no longer present.

"I always visualize," Brice said. "Kelly actually taught me that. Just visualize making plays. First couple of plays off the play sheet, just visualize making that play, what defense they'd be in. Even when I was redshirting, I still just visualized me making those plays that they were making, in my head going where the ball should go and things like that and making checks."

Tavien Feaster took it to the 5-yard line on a powerful run, and he ran behind a determined block by Cervenka. Another run by Feaster to the 2, and then in came Etienne for Feaster. On the thirteenth play of the drive, Etienne ran in easily off the right side, and Clemson was up 27–23. They found a way to go 94 yards for the go-ahead score in a bout of survival reminiscent of when they somehow got by N.C. State at home two years earlier. Then freshman end Xavier Thomas and the defense feasted on Dungey on the final possession to end it. Clemson finished the game with 293 rushing yards on 53 carries, Etienne supplying 203 on 27 attempts. The defense yielded just 90 yards in the second half, forcing five Syracuse punts.

"Danny Ford and Gene Stallings are probably drinking a beer and celebrating somewhere right now," Swinney said. "Because that was an old-school—old-school—way of winning a game. But it's what we had to do.… We ran it when they knew we were going to run it, and it was unbelievable."

If you merely looked at the score and didn't pay attention to the details, you probably wondered why Clemson was in such a close game against an inferior team on its home field. But this was so much more than that, and a week of emotional torment was all over the face of Swinney during his postgame press conference. "It's been a long week and it's been a tough week. Challenges within the week, challenges within the game. The game was kind of a reflection of the week. But at the end of the day, it's all about how you respond."

Three weeks earlier, the Tigers had just enough at Texas A&M with Bryant and Lawrence. Now they had just enough without them. Swinney calmed fears of a long-term absence for Lawrence by saying he had minor concussion symptoms and wanted to go back into the game. The Tigers' prized freshman was going to be fine. And so was a team that probably never envisioned having to fight so hard and overcome so much for a 5-0 start.

"I always tell our guys about the heart of a champion, and it's hard to define," Swinney said. "But you just know it when you see it. And you know

Freshman Xavier Thomas crashes into Syracuse quarterback Eric Dungey on the Orange's final possession.

Christian Wilkins hands out donuts at the Tigers' championship parade.

Dabo Swinney and his team in the tunnel before the ACC title game against Pittsburgh.

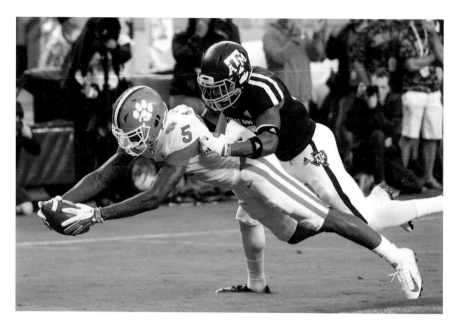

Tee Higgins dives into the end zone after a long catch-and-run for a touchdown at Texas A&M.

The confetti drops on Clemson after its 30–3 spanking of Notre Dame in the Cotton Bowl.

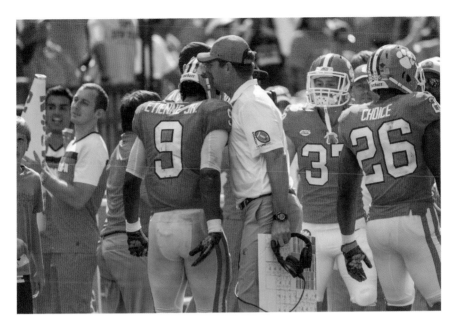

Jeff Scott and Travis Etienne after Etienne scored what proved to be the game-winning touchdown against Syracuse.

Fireworks and the national anthem before the national championship at Levi's Stadium.

Tee Higgins hangs on to a long Trevor Lawrence pass by his fingertips and races for an early touchdown against N.C. State.

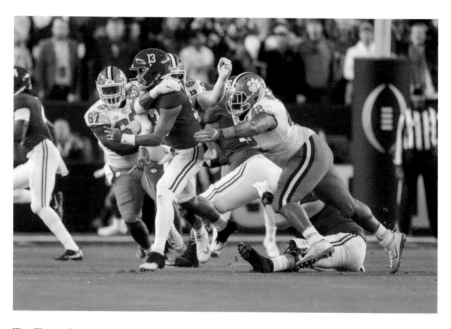

Tua Tagovailoa is swarmed by Clelin Ferrell and Christian Wilkins.

Austin Bryant runs toward the student section before the game against Syracuse.

Trevor Lawrence walks the field before the Cotton Bowl.

Xavier Thomas with a sack of Eric Dungey in the final minute of Clemson's 27–23 win over Syracuse.

Dabo Swinney and his team before the Cotton Bowl.

Travis Etienne breaks loose at Texas A&M.

Brent Venables gets a Gatorade bath late against Pittsburgh.

Justyn Ross leaps high for a pass from Trevor Lawrence against N.C. State.

Players touch Howard's Rock before playing host to Duke.

Hunter Renfrow supplies a big catch-and-run early against N.C. State.

The defensive line poses during the Cotton Bowl celebration.

Derion Kendrick spins for extra yardage against Syracuse.

Clelin Ferrell brings down Tua Tagovailoa on fourth down in the fourth quarter to end Alabama's last threat.

Tee Higgins and the Tigers torched South Carolina via air and ground.

Trevor Lawrence throws at Texas A&M.

Christian Wilkins with some choice words to Alabama's Isaiah Buggs.

The parade route makes its way to Death Valley for the stadium celebration of the 2018 national championship.

Tee Higgins and Justyn Ross at Wake Forest.

Trevor Lawrence celebrates with Christian Wilkins after Wilkins's run for a touchdown at Florida State.

Justyn Ross bobbles and catches a long pass on third down on a third-quarter touchdown drive against Alabama.

Christian Wilkins races to the end zone to celebrate another offensive touchdown at Wake Forest.

Hunter Renfrow with one of the biggest plays of the season, a leaping grab of a Chase Brice throw to convert a third down and set up a field goal in the third quarter against Syracuse.

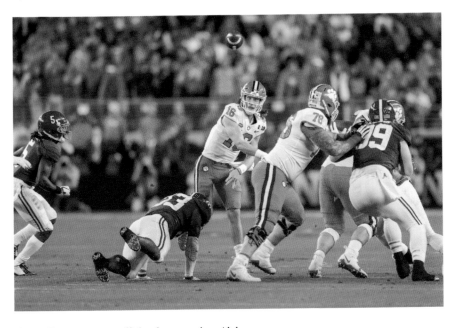

Trevor Lawrence gets off the throw against Alabama.

Hunter Renfrow against South Carolina in his final game at Death Valley.

Brent Venables and his family in the national championship parade.

it when you don't. Man, that's all I can say: The heart of a champion. That's our culture, that's our offseason program, that's the leadership of our team. Everything in life is about how you respond. It's not about what happens great in your life or challenging in your life. It's how you respond. And I've never been more proud of a team in all my life. I've had a lot of unbelievable, great wins as a head coach. I've been a part of some great ones as a player, great ones as an assistant coach in all my years. But I'll never forget this one. This one right here, this one will rank up there with the biggest ones I've ever had. And some people may say, 'Well it's just the fifth game of the year.' But it's more than that. Because I saw a team grow up. I saw a team stand up for each other and have each other's back and just not quit. You know? That's just what it's all about."

CHAPTER 6

LEAP OF FAITH

Awkward silence permeated the living room of C.J. Spiller's home in Lake Butler, Florida, on an evening in late January 2006. Dabo Swinney had basically been laughed at by coaches on his own staff for persisting in his pursuit of Spiller. The top recruit in Florida going to…Clemson? Get real, Dabo.

Running backs coach Burton Burns had already done a bunch of legwork on Terry Grant, a four-star back from Mississippi. Grant was going to be a big get for Clemson, the kind of get the Tigers weren't used to. And now this fanciful notion that Swinney had a prayer of landing this superstar Spiller was threatening to ruin it.

Swinney was so confident that he brought Tommy Bowden to Lake Butler for an in-home visit. Swinney knew how much Spiller loved his trip to Clemson, when James Davis and Jacoby Ford hosted him. He knew what almost no one else knew: that Spiller was probably going to be a Tiger. Even without having ever witnessed a Clemson football game.

This night of January 22, when Spiller returned from a visit to Miami, was when Spiller was going to tell the head coach he was a silent commit to Clemson. Except he never did. Not that night. "I hadn't told nobody where I was going," Spiller said. "Didn't tell my mom. Didn't tell any friends. I was like, 'No, I want to surprise my mom.'"

After Bowden hopped into the rental car, Swinney pulled aside Spiller and pressed him. Spiller indicated to Swinney he was coming, but Bowden still wasn't sold. A few days later, Bowden and Burns were about to get on

C.J. Spiller, before the national championship against Alabama on January 7, 2019. *By Maddie Williams.*

a plane to see Grant in Mississippi. Bowden called Spiller. "I think Terry Grant was getting ready to make his commitment to Clemson," Spiller recalled. "Coach Bowden said, 'Listen, are you coming to Clemson?' I still remember saying, 'Coach. Do not get on that plane. I'm coming to Clemson.' He said OK."

This was but one of several dramatic, fateful, pivotal moments that would unfold involving Spiller over the next three tumultuous years. The type of stuff that seems better fit for a movie script than reality. It's almost impossible to disagree with the following statement: C.J. Spiller is the most important player in Clemson football history. Because if you believe the current era is the foremost era in Clemson football history, then you have to believe Dabo Swinney is the foremost coach in Clemson football history. "I would call C.J. Spiller the founding father of what Clemson football is today," said Tim Bourret, Clemson's longtime sports information director, who retired in April 2018.

If there's no Spiller at Clemson, there's probably none of this. Spiller's presence at Clemson helped open the pathway for other celebrated players to come to the foothills of South Carolina from other parts of the country. In 2009, Swinney had merely a vision to sell Tajh Boyd as more decorated coaches from Ohio State, Tennessee and Oregon pursued the acclaimed quarterback from Hampton Roads, Virginia. In 2011, a program-changing receiver from Fort Myers, Florida, was sold on the notion that he could help reverse the fortunes of a 6-7 season in 2010. Boyd and Sammy Watkins played integral roles in the instant revitalization of Clemson's offense, and from there it wasn't as hard for Swinney and his staff to recruit.

Terry Don Phillips is justifiably given credit for what he saw in Swinney when he was a receivers coach, seeing enough to take a chance on him in 2008 when most everyone on the outside (and surely some on the inside) were wondering what the hell he was doing. But Phillips's gamble was not the only gamble that set this thing, this bordering-on-fairytale Decade of Dabo, in motion. Spiller took quite a gamble himself, dating to the moment he first met Swinney in 2005. Swinney came down to Union County High School to see Kevin Alexander, who would commit to Clemson. Swinney wanted to speak with Spiller, so someone went and pulled Spiller out of class and told him: "The coach from Clemson wants to see you and talk to you." Spiller thought sure, why not. A good excuse to get out of this boring class. They were in the field house at Union County—Spiller, Swinney and Spiller's teammate Mathis Jackson. Swinney asked Spiller if he'd come visit Clemson. Spiller said yes. "He really didn't believe me," Spiller said. "He thought it was a joke. I'm pretty sure the coaches at Clemson were telling him he was wasting his time doing all this stuff. So he didn't believe me."

Swinney whipped out a business card and asked Spiller to sign under a makeshift contract saying he would visit Clemson. "He was like, 'Sign it,'" Spiller said. "'I want to make sure you're going to follow through with your word.' Sure enough, me, him and Mathis Jackson signed that little card saying I would visit Clemson. I think it kind of shocked him a little bit. Like, 'Oh, shoot. Really?'"

This was only the first of several momentous decisions by Spiller, rolls of the dice to take the road less traveled, that bring goosebumps in hindsight. Fast-forward past the signing-day announcement for Clemson that shocked college football and angered his mother. Skip through the 2006 season, Spiller's first, one that had such promise when the Tigers went to Tallahassee and knocked off Florida State, followed by the Thunder (Davis) and Lightning (Spiller) showcase against Georgia Tech back when having

ESPN *GameDay* on campus was an intoxicating novelty all by itself. Go to the end of that season, when everything went off the rails with four losses in the last five games after a 7-1 start. Spiller was devastated after South Carolina came into Death Valley and grabbed a 31–28 win. Then he was angry and confused and disillusioned after he and Davis had a total of 13 carries in a Music City Bowl loss to Kentucky.

The team down the road from his hometown would go on to claim a national title in Urban Meyer's second season. Back home, Spiller felt the pull from the Gators. He started to think about the possibilities of playing in an offense with Tim Tebow and Percy Harvin. Tebow was there when Spiller paid a visit to Florida's campus. When Spiller hopped in his car to make the six-hour drive back to Clemson, it was going to be his last drive back to Clemson. He was going there to pack up his apartment. He was going to be a Gator.

"Me and Coach Swinney went for a little ride when I got back," Spiller said. "He talked about emotions and frustrations, and don't ever make a decision when you're frustrated because you're not really thinking clearly. Coach always says it best: You just bloom where you're planted. Why go in somebody else's backyard when you can have your own backyard? That's what he told me. And it kind of made sense."

Back in January 2016, in Glendale when Clemson was taking on Alabama the first time, Spiller was on the sideline, and he saw Meyer. Meyer gave him a playful jab and told him he was still mad he didn't get him. He told Spiller he was the only guy he really wanted at Florida who got away. Spiller told him, "Well, I guess you didn't recruit me good enough, like Coach Swinney."

So Spiller stayed, through 2007 and then through that 2008 midseason craziness when Swinney took over, and then through December when Swinney became the guy for good. If Spiller is healthy against Wake Forest and plays that whole game and the Tigers win, what happens? Bowden probably isn't out four days later, and who the heck knows. What happens if, in January 2009, Spiller decides to go to the NFL a year early? He was sitting in his car outside the McFadden Building that day, about a half hour before the press conference. His mother, and plenty of others from home, wanted him to go. He told her he was staying, hung up on her and then walked into Swinney's office crying.

"All he did was hug me," Spiller said. "He was like, 'Hey, you can't base this decision off other people's opinions and thoughts, even the ones closest to you. You have to make the decision based off what you feel and what you think is best in your heart.' We really just talked about graduation. I was so close to graduating. Coach said, 'Why give up that opportunity when you can do it and also have a chance to play one more season?'"

Spiller walked out of the room without saying what he was going to do, across the hall into the auditorium packed with all those people. "I think he was still kind of nervous about what I was going to do because I never said yes or no," Spiller said of Swinney. "I just said, 'You're right.' I just went up there and did it."

He stayed. And without him Clemson probably doesn't win the Atlantic Division title in 2009. And if that doesn't happen, what happens in 2010 when the Tigers go 6-7? What in the world was Dabo Swinney thinking when he, and he only, had the crazy idea that a talent like Spiller would leave Florida and come to Clemson?

This.

CHAPTER 7

LEAVE NO DOUBT

I n two of its first five games of the 2018 season, Clemson had to give everything it had just to survive. This was not part of the plan entering the season for fans, who were set on the Tigers plundering through the regular season with little resistance. They were fortunate at Texas A&M, and they were fortunate at home against Syracuse.

This was irksome to orange-clad scoreboard watchers who saw other supposedly elite teams racking up the style points. On top of ripping Louisville to shreds by a 51–14 score in the opener, Alabama had beaten that same Texas A&M team by 22 points. Georgia went to South Carolina and physically mauled the Gamecocks in a 41–17 beatdown. The Crimson Tide and Bulldogs were the two main objects of interest to Clemson fans after the two teams played for a national title the year before. Georgia was recruiting like gangbusters under third-year coach Kirby Smart, making some think the Bulldogs might be surpassing the Tigers.

Winning alone is enough to satisfy plenty of fans who remember when getting to ten wins seemed almost unattainable under Tommy Bowden. But another faction wants ruthless pillaging every game, to step on the other team's throat and not let up. A week after the survival against Syracuse, the Tigers began making the latter group happy when Trevor Lawrence and the offense found a rhythm.

Once upon a time, Florida State encountered feeble resistance in the 1990s when it joined the ACC and found itself existing with a bunch of basketball schools and a football school (Clemson) mired in mediocrity. The

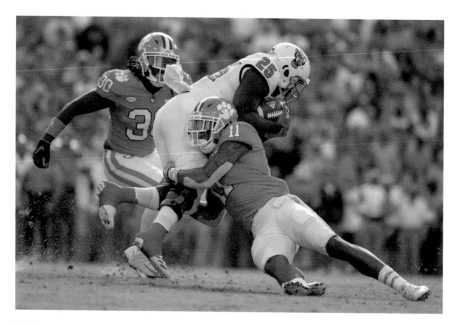

Isaiah Simmons and Clemson's defense shut down a Wolfpack offense that scored 31 against the Tigers the year before.

ascendant Seminoles were at their blistering best in that era, amassing a 70-2 record in ACC games at one point and extending their streak of Top 5 AP finishes to a staggering fourteen consecutive years while collecting two national titles.

In a more recent era—as in, five years ago—Clemson was a really good program that was still looking up at Florida State. The Seminoles dominated the ACC from 2012 to 2014, winning all three ACC titles and the 2013 national title. But then it all started falling apart with a loss at Georgia Tech in 2015, snapping the Seminoles' 28-game ACC winning streak. Florida State still won 10 games in 2015 and 2016, but foundational cracks were apparent, and then it all came crashing down in 2017 when the Seminoles finished 7-6 and Jimbo Fisher left for Texas A&M. So at present, the ACC looks a lot like it did in the 1990s. Except Clemson is doing the dominating and Florida State is trying to make itself relevant again.

Ten years ago, Wake Forest was a major threat to Clemson and the last banana peel Bowden slipped on before parting with the school. Losing to the Demon Deacons hastened Ken Hatfield's firing in 1993, and the same was true of Bowden in 2008. A resounding win over Wake in Dabo Swinney's first season was the spark that turned a 2-3 start into an Atlantic Division title in 2009. The streak over the Deacons was at nine games entering the 2018 trip to Winston-Salem.

The offense had trouble getting going early, but it didn't really matter because the defense kept stifling the Deacons and getting the ball back to Lawrence and Co. Travis Etienne broke through for a 59-yard touchdown run with 6:25 left in the first quarter after two punts and a lost fumble. The floodgates thus opened on a brutal rushing assault that piled up 471 yards in the 63–3 mauling. Clemson hadn't rushed for this much since a 536-yard day against Wake Forest in 1981. The method of this domination was viewed as a tribute to former Tiger running back C.J. Fuller, who had died a few days before at the age of twenty-two after a blood clot related to a recent knee surgery. Three Tigers rushed for at least 125 yards apiece for the first time in school history as Clemson improved to 6-0. Etienne had 167 yards and three touchdowns. Freshman Lyn-J Dixon rushed for 163 yards and two scores, and Adam Choice had 128 yards and a touchdown.

Lawrence looked just fine after coming back from his neck strain. He completed 20 of 25 passes for 175 yards, including a 55-yard scoring strike to Justyn Ross. Wake Forest finished with 175 rushing yards, but that total in no way told the story of how much Clemson's defense throttled the Deacons; when Clemson was up 35–0 just 75 seconds into the third quarter, Wake had minus-2 yards rushing.

Clemson began the season ranked No. 2 in the AP poll behind Alabama. But the tight games against Texas A&M and Syracuse had downgraded the Tigers to No. 4 entering the Wake Forest game as Georgia and then Ohio State moved up. But the annihilation of the Deacons showed that Clemson could pile on the style points, too. N.C. State was next after an open date, and the week off came at a great time because it gave Swinney and his staff extra time to make the team stew over what had happened the previous two seasons.

The Wolfpack gave the Tigers all they could handle both years. In 2016, a missed chip-shot field goal by N.C. State kept Clemson alive, and the Tigers won in overtime. In 2017, the Tigers' defense was hanging on by a thread early and late before K'Von Wallace ended the threat with a sensational pass breakup and then an interception. Those two results suggested these programs were on even terms. N.C. State and its sixth-year coach, Dave Doeren, certainly felt that way and said so. N.C. State's offensive line more than held its own against Clemson's celebrated defensive front in both games. Swinney had an extra week to stoke those motivational fires, to remind his prideful defensive linemen that the Wolfpack had gotten the better of them in back-to-back years. This was being called the "game of the year" in the ACC, yet Clemson was favored by 17 points.

N.C. State was 5-0 and the first ranked opponent Clemson had faced since Alabama in the Sugar Bowl the previous season. The Wolfpack had seasoned quarterback Ryan Finley and a diverse group of receivers who were difficult to cover the year before in Carter-Finley Stadium. To many observers, this game was going to be a war because the previous two were wars. But the Tigers were coming with their vengeful best for this one, and they completely outclassed Doeren's team in a 41–7 bloodletting that was basically over at halftime with Clemson up 24–0.

Doeren came in saying his team just had to make one or two more plays to finally knock off Clemson. They were about two hundred plays away in this one. A white-knuckle affair was far from a given. This was more of the brass-knuckle variety as eighty-five Clemson players got on the field. "There was a real edge to this group all week," Swinney said. "They were eager to get back to work....You're getting ready to play an undefeated team, at home, homecoming, all that stuff. It's a lot of fun."

The defensive line pillaged. The secondary smothered. Lawrence and the receivers did just about whatever they wanted, including a gorgeous 46-yard strike from Lawrence to Tee Higgins that made it 14–0 in the first quarter. So many people spent the week wondering why the spread was so high at 17 points. So many people walked out of the stadium wondering why it wasn't higher. The 34-point margin was deceptive. If not for the goal-line offense and field-goal team messing up a couple of opportunities in the first half, it would have been worse. N.C. State crossed midfield just once in the first half. At halftime, the Tigers had 289 yards to N.C. State's 100 and 16 first downs to the Pack's four.

Linebacker Isaiah Simmons said the entire team took exception to State's players and coaches saying Clemson "escaped" the previous two years against the Wolfpack. "We took this game personal because of all the things they've been saying this week. We wanted to make sure there wasn't a question."

Or leave no doubt, as Swinney is prone to saying. The no-doubt tour continued the next week in Tallahassee, a place that used to make Clemson fans tremble with fear. On this trip, they were giddy with anticipation as they bought up tickets Florida State fans didn't want. In each of the previous three meetings with the Seminoles, Clemson was regarded as the better team. But all three were fourth-quarter games, including in 2017, when FSU

Trevor Lawrence takes off for a run early against N.C. State.

was within 17–14 and had the ball in Clemson territory with 6:36 left in the game (Clemson rebounded and won 31–14).

This was a chance to send first-year coach Willie Taggart a message as he tried to get a grip on the reeling Seminoles program. And after a 0–0 first quarter, Clemson commenced a beatdown that was far worse than the 59–10 score indicated. A 28-point second quarter and a 24-point third quarter turned the TV and social-media focus to a shirtless FSU professor who spent the second half in the stands reading a book titled *Dark Places*. Lawrence and his receivers effortlessly carved up Florida State's flailing secondary. The defense forced seven three-and-outs and collected 14 tackles for loss, including 5 sacks. The staff was able to use this game to get the reserves in early and let them gain experience. "Just a great opportunity to continue to develop your entire roster," said defensive coordinator Brent Venables.

He said this not after a game against Furman but a game against Florida State. At Florida State. For the Seminoles, it tied a 1973 defeat to Florida for the worst loss in school history. It was also Clemson's fourth consecutive win over FSU. A month earlier, Clemson had considered itself enormously fortunate to leave its own stadium with a 4-point win over Syracuse. The Tigers won their next three games by a combined score of 163–20, and

Hunter Renfrow reaches for a Trevor Lawrence pass at Florida State.

this barrage showed that Clemson could beat people's brains in just like Alabama was doing.

It also showed that Swinney made the right call to go with Lawrence as the starter after four games. The freshman was establishing himself as an exceedingly rare talent with his rocket arm and poise far beyond his years. As it turned out, Kelly Bryant probably did everyone a favor by leaving when he did because it eliminated any hint of controversy and set a more rapid course toward Lawrence becoming more confident and taking ownership of the team.

"Kelly was one of my best friends on the team," senior tight end Milan Richard reflected later. "I feel like he and I grew up a lot that previous year, both stepping into starting roles. So I definitely wanted him to stay. I think he would've helped this team in the locker room, just helping us maintain the leadership of the team and everything that needed to go on. But I think him deciding to go ahead and leave maybe did help Trevor, because he wasn't really worried about the going back and forth between the two guys. When Kelly made that decision, he did what was best for him. So I'm never going to be mad at him for doing what he felt was best for him. But I do think it gave Trevor the freedom and a little bit of relief to kind of go ahead and take the keys to the team. And we told him that as an offense. Some of the older guys said, 'Hey listen: We're behind you. It's your team now. Do your thing and we're behind you 100 percent.' So I do think it ended up working out better for Trevor emotionally because Kelly decided to go ahead and transfer."

Elsewhere, supposed juggernauts were looking a lot more human. Georgia suffered a 36–16 thrashing at LSU on October 13, the week before Clemson's romp over N.C. State. Ohio State had gone to Purdue and fallen apart in a 49–20 disaster. Clemson was back to No. 2 in the AP poll, right behind Alabama. The Tigers' trail of destruction continued the next week in Death Valley when they smashed hapless Louisville 77–16 and hastened the firing of Bobby Petrino. But later that night, the team from Tuscaloosa took all the limelight by turning a highly anticipated showdown at LSU into a 29–0 soul-crusher of the Bayou Bengals.

Earlier in the season, Bill Bender of the *Sporting News* wrote it was "clear" that Alabama and Ohio State were on a collision course. Now, Rodger Sherman of The Ringer wrote that the terrifying Tide's only worthy 2018 opponent was going to be history:

> *And this year, Alabama isn't just good: It's dominating college football to an extent that even past Alabama teams haven't. Maybe this makes the 2018 season a horror show. Many have complained that the Tide's year-in, year-out success has made the sport uninteresting. And in that sense, this season is worse than most.*
>
> *To me, though, this Alabama squad is significantly more entertaining than any prior team coached by Nick Saban. In the past, Bama's dominance was too workmanlike to love. It won by shutting down opposing offenses and scoring just enough points to make clear the game wasn't close. Take its BCS championship demolition of LSU, for example. The Tide's quarterbacks have often been called "game managers" for their ability to avoid turnovers rather than showcase any special talents. The Tide's running backs have bludgeoned their way to two Heisman Trophy wins since 2009.*
>
> *With Tagovailoa at quarterback, however, Alabama has unlocked a new level of offense—and a new level of dominance. If Alabama ends the season as it's started it, the 2018 Tide won't just go down as the best team in college football this season. They could go down as the greatest college football team of all time....*
>
> *The present sports discourse is obsessed with debating whether a player is the greatest of all time. LeBron James can't dribble without being*

Defensive end Xavier Thomas made a splash in 2018 as a freshman.

compared with Michael Jordan. Sunday Night Football *dressed up live goats in Tom Brady and Aaron Rodgers jerseys to celebrate the two players facing off in New England over the weekend. Everything has to be GOAT-related. (I have partaken in the discourse.)*

And yet here we have Alabama, legitimately in the running to be considered the greatest college football team of all time, and many fans consider it a massive turnoff. The Tide are making the season irrelevant, because it's so obvious that they're going to win it all....

It's undeniable that Alabama is sucking some of the intrigue out of this college football season. If you thought oddsmakers' 14.5-point spread in Bama-LSU was stunning, take a look at Bovada's preliminary betting lines for the Tide's most likely potential playoff opponents. They would be favored by nine points against Clemson, 14.5 points against Michigan, and a whopping 21 points against Notre Dame. Think about that: There's just one team in the country that seems likely to come within 10 points of Alabama. If all that matters is whether Alabama outplays its opponents on the field every week, this season is dull. But it's fascinating to watch Alabama try to outplay the ghosts of legends past. Can the Tide really make it through the entire season without playing a close game?

CHAPTER 8

THE PHONE CALL

I t was a Thursday in January 2012, and the foremost item on Dabo
Swinney's mind was the upcoming recruiting weekend. Everyone on
the outside was preoccupied with the search to replace Kevin Steele,
but that deal was almost done. To this day, Swinney won't name the guy he'd
targeted, but that doesn't matter. When Swinney drove home that evening,
in his pocket was a cellphone number Terry Don Phillips had given him.
The name beside that number: Brent Venables.

A thorough examination of ten years of Dabo and how all this came to
be—the stupendous, surreal, unimaginable success of recent years—has to
include the story of how Venables came to Clemson. Or, more precisely, what
had to happen for him to come to Clemson. It's yet another mystical layer in
this too-movie-to-be-true era. It's also yet another example of Phillips, who
saw something in Swinney when Tommy Bowden walked, setting in motion
something momentous.

Go back to that fall of 2008, after Bowden was out and Swinney was in.
Phillips surprised everyone by pointing at Swinney that October 13 day in
the McFadden conference room and telling him he was the interim guy. The
AD told Swinney he wanted him to succeed, that this thirty-eight-year-old
receivers coach had what Clemson needed. But he also told Swinney and
everyone else he was going to hire the best coach he could find. And so he
set out on a search while Swinney was going through his six-game audition.

Message boards were in a tizzy on November 11, three days after Swinney's
team lost 41–27 at Florida State, when Internet sleuths discovered that

Clemson's university plane was headed to Oklahoma. Phillips was going to interview Bob Stoops. That was the conclusion made by a segment of fans. Hey, Stoops was interested in the Clemson job back when he was a Florida assistant and the Tigers were looking for a replacement for Tommy West. So it made perfect sense, right? Well, no. The reality: Phillips was not-so-secretly meeting with Stoops's defensive coordinator at the airport in Oklahoma City. The reality was also that Phillips, familiar with Venables from his days as the athletics director at Oklahoma State, was enormously impressed when the meeting concluded. "I had a great interview with Brent," Phillips said in the fall of 2018. "Which, frankly, created a difficult decision."

Everyone knows what happened thereafter. Swinney showed Phillips what he wanted to see by going 4-2 and bringing new energy to the team and the fan base. Much less known is what happened three years later, after the West Virginia debacle in the Orange Bowl. That atrocity, plus a third consecutive loss to South Carolina, had Swinney on the defensive with fans and media. The season was being called a failure, which really ticked him off because just a month earlier he'd delivered the first ACC title in decades. All the euphoria from that 8-0 start, with Sammy Watkins and Tajh Boyd and Chad Morris, wasn't all just washed away by what happened at the end.

Brent Venables with Mike Reed (*left*) and Lemanski Hall (*center*).

That's what he reminded everyone. He also laughed at the suggestion that it would take years to recover from that massacre in South Florida. Swinney got rid of Steele not solely because of the 70-spot but because it was just not working. Kind of like a bad marriage. He had his list of candidates after the parting with Steele, and then he had his guy. Again, he won't say who. Again, it doesn't really matter.

Venables was in a sticky situation at Oklahoma. The fans were ticked that the Sooners had been lit up that year by several sensational offenses in the Big 12. And Stoops brought in his brother Mike, who'd been fired as Arizona's head coach, to be co–defensive coordinator with Venables. It sure looked like a bit of a demotion for Venables. And though Venables has never publicly confirmed this, it had to feel like one too.

This led him to think about maybe seeing what was out there, possibly leaving his comfort zone and trying something new after thirteen years under Bob Stoops in Norman. He'd watched Clemson from afar and liked what he saw. He was intrigued when he saw how Swinney coached, how Swinney wasn't afraid to be himself and yell and scream in those postgame interviews on the field. There was a joy to Swinney's style that made Venables smile. Venables didn't know Swinney. But he knew the guy who interviewed him for the Clemson job back in 2008 at the Oklahoma City airport.

"I was kind of down the road on a different path," Swinney said. "Terry Don just brought me a note. He said, 'Hey look, do with it what you want to. But Brent reached out to me and said he'd be interested in talking to you if you are interested. He said he likes watching y'all every time you're on TV.' I told Terry Don, 'I'm kind of on a different path here. But I'll give him a call. I appreciate that.' So I just kind of put his cellphone number in my pocket."

Swinney got home that Thursday night, thinking more about the recruiting weekend than anything. He told his wife, Kathleen, that he was going to call this Venables guy from Oklahoma and the chat probably wouldn't take long. That was at about nine o'clock that night. "We talked for three hours," Swinney said. "Literally three hours. I mean, Kath was out there for a little while, but then she was gone to bed. It was three hours of conversation."

By the end of the call, Swinney was smitten. He told Venables that he and his wife, Julie, needed to come to Clemson and see the place. The next night, Venables and his wife were in Clemson. The football team had just wrapped up its end-of-season banquet at the Madren Center near campus when Swinney walked to the lobby of the adjoining Martin Inn to welcome them as they checked in. By the end of the weekend, Venables felt this was

Brent Venables arrived at Clemson in 2012, replacing Kevin Steele after Clemson allowed 70 points to West Virginia in the Orange Bowl.

the move he needed to make. But the decision was still gut-wrenching. He still had to go back to Norman to tell his boss, a guy he basically considered family, that he was leaving. He also had to deal with Swinney telling him he couldn't bring any assistant coaches. If he took this job, he was coming all by himself. "It was a crazy situation, because I loved my staff," Swinney said. "Ain't no way I was getting rid of Marion Hobby and Dan Brooks and Charlie Harbison and those guys."

Talk about a leap of faith for Venables and his family. Clemson might as well have been on Mars. Here's what Swinney told him that weekend: "No, you don't get to bring nobody. I hire everybody. Nobody hires anybody here but me. We've got to understand that right out of the gate. And you'll thank me later. Because these are all great men and great coaches."

Swinney now: "It's been kind of neat to watch that all transpire, because he loves our staff."

And the staff loves being at Clemson. Venables, who has been at the school for seven full seasons, is a microcosm of the remarkable run of staff stability under Swinney. He left Oklahoma to get out of his comfort zone, to experience something new and to prepare himself to be a head coach. And he wasn't exactly the hottest commodity at the time, as plenty of Sooners fans wanted to help him pack his bags after his defense struggled to contain elite offenses in 2011.

Steele hated dealing with the new-age offenses that were proliferating in 2010 and 2011. Venables, who schemed against a multitude of offensive styles at Oklahoma, was ready to take on any and every schematic challenge. His defense began to grow up late in 2012, was hard to handle in 2013 and then became utterly dominant in 2014. Not much has changed since, and Venables has become known as arguably the top assistant in college football. He's been approached for numerous head-coaching jobs but is exceptionally choosy because he savors his current situation. He's well compensated, making more than $2 million a year, and his eldest son, Jake, was a freshman linebacker for the Tigers in 2018. During the spring, he's a regular at his daughters' youth softball games. He is a staunch believer in Swinney's family-driven approach, an ethos that is not confined to grinding away but also includes fun and enjoying the moment and including the family at all turns.

"It's a very close-knit staff," Venables said. "It's just kind of a philosophy of his in regard to team-building, staff-building, if you will. Just got great cohesion, chemistry, respect, appreciation for one another, appreciation for everyone in the building and the job they do....It creates a great environment to make a living in a profession that's very demanding. He makes it really enjoyable....Dabo brings out the very best in everybody. As he says, he's an over-believer. It's not just for the players but for all of us. He creates a sense of belief, but he also creates the accountability and the structure that we all need in order to have consistent success. But he's very genuine and authentic in every day. He knows all the kids on staff. He knows the families very well. He's just a—he's a real special guy."

While Nick Saban's assistant-coach positions are a regular turnstile, Swinney has enjoyed remarkable stability on his sideline. Morris left for the SMU job in 2014. Two years later, he lost his two defensive line coaches when Brooks retired and Hobby left for the Jacksonville Jaguars. So that's three coaches lost over six years. Saban lost six after the 2017 season alone and then five immediately after the 2018 season concluded. Celebrated freshman receiver Justyn Ross said the low turnover on Clemson's staff was the main reason he spurned the home-state Crimson Tide for the Tigers in February 2018.

Venables isn't the only assistant who's been in no hurry to leave. In December 2017, co–offensive coordinator Tony Elliott was pursued by Mississippi State and UCF for their head-coaching jobs. Neither school got far, in part because Elliott believed he needed more seasoning to be a head coach. A year later, the Georgia Tech and North Carolina jobs came open, and Elliott would have been interested in those. But the Yellow Jackets hired Geoff Collins from Temple, and North Carolina brought back old hero Mack Brown.

"I still have a lot of apprehension about it," Elliott said. "It's because I'm focusing on my job. I haven't really put in a lot of time thinking about what it would look like or what my plan would be as a head coach. I'm confident in my ability to go lead a program. I've got the best example in college football [in Swinney]. I know the structure would be very similar. But I just haven't dedicated the time to put my plan together. So that's what I mean when I say I feel like I'm not prepared. I just really haven't been focusing on it because I've been focusing on trying to get better as an offensive coordinator."

In recent years, co–offensive coordinator Jeff Scott has been approached by multiple lower-level FBS schools about head-coaching jobs. But his situation is so good at Clemson that it would take a higher-profile job to pry him away. Scott's name is also popular when major offensive coordinator jobs open up, including Tennessee and Miami in 2018 and Auburn in 2017. Not long after Scott said no thanks to Tennessee's Jeremy Pruitt, Georgia offensive coordinator Jim Chaney took the Volunteers' job for a reported salary of $1.5 million. Scott and Elliott both made $850,000 a year in 2018.

"The way that Coach Swinney treats myself and Tony really as true co-coordinators and not a title, it's really put myself in a position where I don't need to leave to be the play-caller," Scott said. "I feel like I can be a coordinator right here at Clemson. I think at that point when you kind of eliminate other offensive coordinator opportunities it really kind of makes it streamline to being patient and waiting for the right head-coaching opportunity....Tony and I work together very well. Coach Swinney treats us great....My next move out of Clemson will be one day if I get an opportunity to be a head coach. I'm not really looking for opportunities to go anywhere to be a sole coordinator or sole play-caller."

Early in his head-coaching tenure, Swinney was dinged for staff instability. He immediately fired offensive coordinator Rob Spence upon getting the interim job in 2008 and parted ways with defensive coordinator Vic Koenning two months later. In December 2010, he fired offensive coordinator Billy Napier and running backs coach Andre Powell. Then, after the 70–33 nightmare against West Virginia in the 2011 Orange Bowl, he fired Steele.

Morris was selective about other opportunities over his four-year offensive coordinator stint before leaving for SMU. Swinney hired from within to replace him; Scott has been with Swinney since the beginning in 2008, and Elliott replaced Powell in 2011. Tight ends and special teams coach Danny Pearman has been at Clemson since late 2008. Robbie Caldwell has coached the Tigers' offensive line for eight seasons.

Clemson's assistants are all well compensated, so that's a big factor but not the only one. The school also boasts extraordinary harmony and alignment up and down the chain of command—from Swinney, to athletics director Dan Radakovich, to president Jim Clements, to the Board of Trustees. If big egos got in the way, it could all fall apart. Instead, this seems like one big happy family.

"They just have tremendous, tremendous cohesion and respect for one another," Venables said. "There's few other programs out there in college football that are like that, or even in other sports. I use sports as an example. Or you can use businesses. It's no different. When you have that cohesion and the respect and love and appreciation for one another, you can do special things."

Oklahoma still hasn't been able to get things right on defense since Venables's departure seven years ago. Lincoln Riley fired Mark Stoops in the middle of the 2018 season, and the Sooners' defense didn't get any better from there; a few Oklahoma stops of Alabama in the Orange Bowl, and

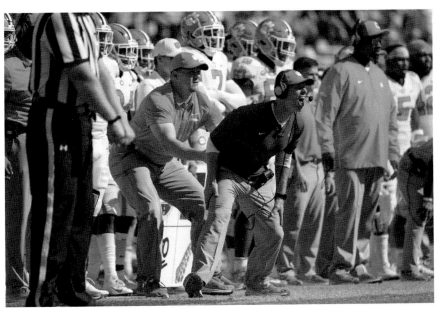

Brent Venables is pulled back to the sideline by his "Get-Back Coach," Adam Smotherman.

Clemson might have been playing the Sooners and not Alabama in the CFP title game. Defense has been the Sooners' main problem since Venables left. Elite defense has been the main constant during Clemson's rise to greatness under Swinney.

And it all started in an Oklahoma airport when Phillips was interviewing a coach for the job Swinney wanted. Not Bob Stoops. Some guy named Brent Venables, the guy whose cell number was in Swinney's pocket that 2012 day when he thought he'd already found his guy.

You can't make this stuff up.

"One day I'm going to write a book and people ain't going to believe it," Swinney said. "It'll be a fun story one of these days. It'll be a great read, no doubt about it."

As if it's not already.

CHAPTER 9

FOUR THE WIN

I n 2015 and 2016, Clemson mastered the art of living dangerously. Five games were decided by 8 points or fewer in the former breakthrough season. A staggering eight contests were decided by the same margin when the Tigers won the national title. The only two losses: 45–40 in the 2015 national title game and 43–42 at home to Pitt in 2016. Late high-wire acts were the rule in those days, when Deshaun Watson and his star-studded cast seemed to relish playing their best when the moment was biggest. The 2016 offense seemed to live for that late game-sealing drive. The 2017 team had just three games decided by 8 or fewer, largely because of a defense that smothered just about everyone.

Dabo Swinney's tenth season became so much different after the pulse-pounding wins over Texas A&M and Syracuse over the first five games. The rest of the ACC was not the same as it was in 2016, when the Tigers had to hold on for dear life in the second half against Lamar Jackson and Louisville. An exodus of high-level quarterbacks put the conference in rebuilding mode. Florida State was reeling but still formidable during Clemson's title run two years earlier, when the Tigers overcame a sensational night from Dalvin Cook in a 37–34 thriller at Doak Campbell Stadium. Now the 2018 Seminoles were an absolute mess on the way to a 5-7 record in Willie Taggart's first season.

When the conference gets worse and Clemson gets better, it adds up to much less suspense. That's a good thing for Clemson and its faithful, but it's also a weird feeling for fans to spend the day tailgating with almost zero worries about losing. If 2015 and 2016 were about the team bringing its own guts and the fans losing theirs, this season was about bringing your own books to read if you got bored—certainly for at least one opposing fan, and possibly for some Clemson supporters as well.

The Louisville game on November 3 was the most surreal example of this suspenseless phenomenon. Since the Cardinals' first year in the ACC in 2014, Clemson fans were accustomed to getting all they could handle from Bobby Petrino's team. The Tigers didn't win as much as survive the first three meetings, by scores of 23–17, 20–17 and then the epic 42–36 triumph over the Jackson-led team in 2016. The script began to change in 2017 when Clemson went to Louisville for a primetime game that was the site of ESPN's *College GameDay* program. Where most people saw it as a perfect opportunity for Jackson and Petrino to finally get back at a team in rebuilding mode on offense, Clemson saw it as a chance to flex its muscle and showcase the growing gap between the two programs. The Tigers chased most of the fans home early that night in a 47–21 pounding.

Without Jackson in 2018, Petrino's team fell apart. The Cardinals' only wins over the entire season came against Indiana State and Western Kentucky. Clemson embarked on the entirely predictable exercise of devouring the Cardinals in a 77–16 mismatch, the largest margin of an ACC victory in school history (surpassing the 60-point win over Wake Forest a month earlier). The running game continued to feast, accounting for 492 of Clemson's 661 total yards. Ten different players combined for the Tigers' 11 touchdowns, and Clemson averaged a school-record 11.6 yards per play. Once upon a time, Petrino and Louisville were viewed with some fear by Clemson fans. When the coach went back to his old school in 2014 after a stint at Western Kentucky, Swinney and his program were in a different place. Successful, yes. But still under the thumb of Florida State, which had smashed the Tigers 51–14 at Death Valley in 2013 on its way to a national title. And still under the hex of Steve Spurrier and South Carolina, which had beaten Clemson five consecutive times. Five years ago, Petrino was viewed as a better coach than Swinney and another difficult obstacle in the ACC's Atlantic Division. A little more than a week after Clemson hung 77 on Petrino, he was fired. His record against Swinney: 0-5.

For Clemson, the only casualty of a weak year for the ACC was the cost in national perception. The first playoff rankings of the season were released two days after the massacre of Florida State, and the national consensus seemed to be that Alabama was a firm No. 1 ahead of Clemson. The Crimson Tide's defense had shown some vulnerability early in the season against Texas A&M and then allowed 31 points to a putrid Arkansas team two weeks later. On November 10, the offensive line struggled to protect Tua Tagovailoa against Mississippi State's high-level defensive front. The next week, the Tide would sleepwalk through the first half against The Citadel and find themselves tied 10–10 with the Bulldogs going to the locker room. But they woke up and took care of business in a 50–17 win, so it seemed to be business as usual in Tuscaloosa.

All along, Dabo Swinney played up the notion that Alabama was in a class of its own. Clemson was on a historic run of domination, and it seemed pretty much accepted by this point that it was the Crimson Tide, Tigers and then everyone else. But the man who'd spent his entire life as an underdog amplified the idea of little ole Clemson considering itself lucky to merely exist in the shadow of Nick Saban's Alabama colossus.

"The reality of it is, back when I was a player we kind of had the big-time bus and then the ROY Bus—the Rest of Y'all," Swinney told ESPN after the first CFP rankings were unveiled. "It is kind of Alabama and the rest of y'all. We are just kind of glad to be on the ROY Bus right now and to still have a chance."

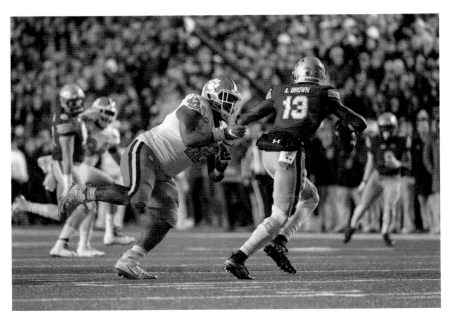

Christian Wilkins knocks quarterback Anthony Brown out of the game at Boston College.

Certainly, most of the national media did not question Clemson's credentials as being better than all but one team. Where in 2015 and 2016 the talking heads still wondered whether this coach and program were the genuine article, now the Tigers were viewed as a certified powerhouse. But Bama's equal? That was a tougher sell. The Crimson Tide supposedly were in a tougher conference. Tagovailoa was viewed as the best player in college football by a wide margin, and the Tide's attacking, star-studded offense was considered unstoppable. Clemson was destroying the competition, too. The Tigers had a great defense and some sensational young offensive weapons of their own. But Alabama had reestablished the natural order of things the previous January in New Orleans, turning back the Clemson uprising with brute force. This new edition of the Tigers, with Trevor Lawrence and Tee Higgins and Travis Etienne and Justyn Ross providing offensive flash that wasn't present in 2017, was fascinating to the college football populace. But there was still widely held doubt about whether the Tigers were fit to go back and forth with Alabama for four quarters as they did two years before.

In recent years, the Tigers have taken great glee in crashing parties, and the trip to Boston College gave them a chance to renew that tradition. ESPN's *College GameDay* originated from Chestnut Hill, and the announcers spent much of the morning wondering how Lawrence and Clemson would handle the cold temperatures. The Tigers privately laughed at those concerns, and then they publicly smothered the Eagles at Alumni Stadium. Christian Wilkins knocked starting quarterback Anthony Brown from the game on the Eagles' first possession, and Boston College's offense couldn't do anything for the rest of the night. A 74-yard punt return for a touchdown brought some buzz to Alumni Stadium with the Eagles up 7–3. But Boston College simply wasn't going to move the ball against this rampaging defense; the Eagles finished with 113 yards of offense and 9 on the ground—216 yards below their season rushing average. Clemson sealed the Atlantic Division for the fourth consecutive year with a 27–7 win, and after celebrating with the fans who made the trip, Swinney mocked the weather topic during his postgame press conference.

"I didn't know what was going to happen listening to all the reports and all this stuff that we were going to forget how to play football....Lord have mercy. But you know, most people didn't do their homework. Since 1961, Clemson is 5-0 in games less than 40 degrees and now 6-0, so I don't know. That's the only thing I was worried about: that we were going to freeze up and forget how to run and tackle and all that stuff. But somehow, some way, we were able to push through it."

Tee Higgins with a catch and run at Boston College.

A week later, at home against Duke, the pregame tailgates outside Death Valley had the usual sense of ease. No one seriously thought that the Blue Devils were going to give Clemson any trouble, but David Cutcliffe's team quieted the crowd early on Military Appreciation Day. The Tigers went three-and-out on their first three possessions. Meanwhile, Duke moved the ball on its second and third possessions and kicked two field goals to take a 6–0 lead after 15 minutes. Clemson shot to life with a seven-play, 75-yard touchdown drive. But then the Tigers punted three more times. A touchdown late in the first half put Clemson up 14–6 at halftime, but fans were wondering what the heck was wrong with all the dropped passes and just 17 rushing yards. On top of that, Hunter Renfrow was out with a concussion after banging his head on the turf diving for a pass. The offense got going in the third with touchdown drives of 61, 75 and 79 yards. And the defense tightened the clamps to keep Duke from scoring again in a 35–6 Clemson victory that pushed the record to 11-0.

The Tigers then shifted their attention to South Carolina and a rivalry game that had turned into a mismatch the previous two years. In 2016, Clemson ripped the Gamecocks apart in a 56–7 trouncing. And in 2017 in Columbia, the beating was much worse than the 34–10 score indicated.

Once upon a time, Steve Spurrier was the enemy of everyone in orange, as he took regular digs at Swinney during South Carolina's five-game winning streak in the series. But then Deshaun Watson ended that streak in 2014 while basically playing on one leg, and everything was different thereafter. Spurrier fell asleep in recruiting, and Clemson's recruiting went from really good to great. Former Florida coach Will Muschamp inherited this when he took over after the 2015 season. Back then he probably didn't envision his chief in-state rival (Clemson) and SEC East rival (Georgia) becoming even better. But that's what happened, and after getting bulldozed by the Bulldogs earlier in the season, Muschamp faced the prospect of going to Clemson's place to take on one of the best two teams in college football.

Tiger fans were giddy at the thought of making it five straight over South Carolina, given how much heartache and agony were suffered when the Gamecocks were on the winning end. The passage of time also enabled Spurrier and Swinney to start liking each other a lot more. In 2017, Spurrier invited Swinney and his wife, Kathleen, to his College Football Hall of Fame induction dinner in New York. Spurrier said there was really no mystery to why Clemson began dominating the rivalry again. The Tigers began looking like an elite team in 2014 and 2015, and the Gamecocks tumbled to mediocrity and worse. From 2011 to 2013, South Carolina went 33-6. Over the next three years, the Gamecocks' record was 16-22. Muschamp's second team went 9-4 in 2017 but then dropped to 7-6 in 2018, capped with a 28–0 loss to Virginia in the Belk Bowl. Since Clemson lost to South Carolina for the fifth straight time in 2013, the Tigers have amassed a 66-7 record and two national titles. The Gamecocks are 33-32 over the same stretch. "I don't think it's too surprising, because Clemson has been beating everybody pretty good," Spurrier said. "So it's difficult for South Carolina to beat those guys. That's just the way it's turned right now."

Where Gamecock fans used to see Spurrier's barbs toward Swinney as confirmation that the Clemson coach was a clown and a fraud, now the South Carolina faithful probably didn't know what to think when learning the Head Ball Coach and Swinney are good buds. "Dabo does a super job, and he does it with class," Spurrier said. "Yeah, I pull for Dabo. Not in this one, of course. But other times—I'm not eaten up with the rivalry because I don't live in South Carolina. But it was a fun rivalry the ten years I coached in it."

On November 24 in Death Valley, Jake Bentley and South Carolina's offense were staring into the jaws of a defense that had gone a long time without allowing a touchdown in a close game. Syracuse, which visited

Dabo Swinney and Will Muschamp before their third meeting.

Clemson on September 29, was the last team to reach the end zone in a non-garbage time situation. The defense had allowed a mere three touchdowns over six games, and all of them came in the fourth quarter of games that had long since been decided. The Gamecocks' offense had done nothing against Clemson in Columbia the year before and nothing in that shellacking two years before. After scoring four touchdowns in the 2015 game in Columbia, South Carolina's offense produced just two over 120 minutes of rivalry football in 2016 and 2017. And both occurred well after matters had been decided: the Gamecocks were down 34–3 in 2017 when they reached the end zone with 2:45 left in the game, and in 2016, they were down 42–0 when they scored a touchdown with 11:24 left in the third quarter.

It was hard to see South Carolina giving Clemson's defense much trouble. And then the Gamecocks gave the Tigers absolute fits. The home fans came wanting nothing less than a massacre, but Bentley and the Gamecocks left the Tigers' secondary bloodied with a stunning 510 yards through the air. Clemson won the game by three touchdowns, and its offense was absolutely unstoppable while totaling 744 yards and 56 points. But that 35 on the other side of the scoreboard was not appealing, and it put a bit of a damper on the celebration of a 12-0 regular season.

"That's about as bad a performance on the back end that we've ever had since I've been here," Swinney said. Brent Venables was genuinely shaken after watching his defense allow Gamecock receivers to run completely free behind his defense. He used words such as "disgusting" and "pathetic" to describe what he saw and said he was embarrassed. The next day, Swinney was shown an article from a Clemson website that quoted a Clemson fan saying the win "felt like a loss." That precise phrasing was in the article's headline, and Swinney went off later in the day during a teleconference to discuss the ACC championship game matchup against Pitt.

"I just want to win by one more point. If that ever gets to where that's not enough, then it's time for me to move on somewhere else. I ain't never going to apologize for a 21-point win over a state rival, ever. You people who suggest it felt like a loss, y'all need to check yourself, too. I've been here sixteen years, and for all those people out there who want to complain about five wins in a row and winning by three touchdowns, man that's shameful. That's a lack of respect for our program and a lack of respect for the effort that these players and coaches put in. I hope you write that. The senior class has won 52 games and we've got people complaining. Give me a break. If 12-0 ain't good enough, then it's time to seek other places. Make sure you get that. I'm going to say it one more time: We've got eight 10-plus win seasons, we're 12-0. It's the third time in the history of this school we've won five state championships in a row. And when that's not enough for some people, that's sad. That's sad."

The rant created a big sensation in the moment. Swinney saw it as an opportunity to forcefully remind everyone just how good life was at Clemson, which had just completed a perfect season while winning for the 55th time its previous 59 games. More than anyone, Swinney also remembered the venom from fans during the 5-game losing streak. Even when defeats to the Gamecocks were rare blemishes on a 10-win season in 2011 and 11-win seasons in 2012 and 2013, some fans said he should be fired for his inability to beat the school in Columbia. Now a faction of people was less than enthused over a three-touchdown win over that same program.

Earlier in the season, Nick Saban created a stir when he called out students for their lack of interest in a game against Louisiana–Lafayette: "When I first came here, you used to play that tradition thing up there and everybody was cheering and excited and happy and there was great spirit. Now they don't even cheer," Saban said on September 29. "They introduce our players, and nobody even cheers. So I don't know, maybe there's something else somebody else ought to talk about. Maybe I shouldn't talk about it. Maybe

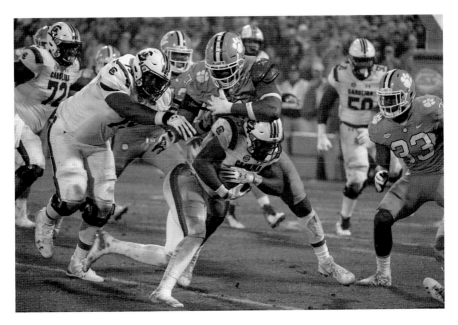

The defense had two major stops with South Carolina close to the Tigers' end zone.

I already talked about it more than I should. So you all can beat me up for that if you want. Look, our players work too hard and they deserve to have everything and people supporting them in every way and have tremendous spirit for what they've done. They may not be able to continue to do it. We're going to work hard to try to continue that. But there's a part of it where other people need to support them too, and there's got to be a spirit that makes it special to play here, because that's what makes it special to be here. And if that's not here, then does it continue to be special to be here or not? That's the question everybody has to ask. I'm asking it right now."

The furor over those comments didn't last long, and neither did the commotion over Swinney's tirade a day after the South Carolina game. The Crimson Tide and Tigers were on a collision course, and that's what ultimately occupied people's minds more than words from the coaches. A couple of hours before Clemson kicked off against South Carolina, Alabama had its hands full with Auburn in the first half in Tuscaloosa. The two teams were on even terms in the first half, after which Alabama had a 17–14 lead. The Tigers hit for some big plays on offense and made moving the ball difficult for a Crimson Tide offense that had also struggled in the first half against The Citadel and Mississippi State the previous two weeks. Alabama

Dexter Lawrence and Clemson's defensive line overwhelmed Pittsburgh in the ACC championship game.

found itself after halftime with 21 third-quarter points and beat Auburn 52–21 on the strength of five touchdown passes from Tua Tagovailoa.

The next week, Clemson's fourth consecutive ACC title was viewed as a formality leading to a game against Pittsburgh at Charlotte's Bank of America Stadium. The Panthers were 7-5 and had been drubbed by Penn State (51–6), UCF (45–14) and Miami (24–3). Clemson removed most suspense early on a field that had been drenched by rain over the entire day, taking a quick 14–0 lead on a 75-yard run by Travis Etienne on the opening play and a fumble return by Christian Wilkins that set up a short scoring run by Etienne. Clemson coasted to a 42–10 win in the soggy conditions, improving to 13-0 and punching its ticket to a fourth consecutive playoff in businesslike fashion. Four consecutive outright conference titles was unprecedented. Florida State didn't do it during its scorched-earth era from 1992 to 2000, nor when Jimbo Fisher lifted the program back to national prominence. Clemson's defense rebounded from the wild night a week earlier against South Carolina, holding Pitt to just 8 passing yards and 199 total yards. Pitt coach Pat Narduzzi, whose team had pushed Notre Dame earlier in the season at South Bend before losing 19–14, was asked to compare the Irish and Tigers.

"There's no comparison. Clemson is the best football team we've played to this point. They deserve to be where they are. They'll probably win a national championship. It's a good football team from the front end to the back end as far as the talent they've got. Dabo has done a great job. Ton of respect for him. Love that guy. Clemson is the measuring stick in the ACC right now."

Clemson secured another ACC crown with a suspense-free evening in Charlotte, winning by 20 or more points for the eighth consecutive game. The drama of the day had already unfolded earlier, 250 miles down I-85 in Atlanta. Georgia had another shot at Alabama inside Mercedes-Benz Stadium after letting a 13–0 halftime lead slip away in the national title game eleven months earlier. The Bulldogs took a 20–10 lead into the fourth quarter of that game, but Tagovailoa rallied the Crimson Tide to overtime and then a 26–23 triumph on a 41-yard touchdown pass to DeVonta Smith.

In the 2018 SEC title game, Alabama was viewed as better than the year before because Tagovailoa's presence made the Tide's offense prolific. Georgia had taken a step back from 2017 after losing transcendent players Nick Chubb, Sony Michel, Roquan Smith and Lorenzo Carter. Nevertheless, the Bulldogs looked to be every bit Alabama's equal for much of the game.

Christian Wilkins returns a fumble early against Pitt.

Georgia had a 21–7 lead in the second quarter and a 28–14 advantage early in the third quarter when Jake Fromm found Riley Ridley for a 23-yard touchdown strike.

Tagovailoa was injured early after taking a shot to his ankle but remained in the game. He made a poor decision early on a pass that was intercepted at the goal line, and in the third quarter, the Bulldogs picked off another of his passes in the end zone. Georgia's offense was effective with both power running by D'Andre Swift and pinpoint downfield passes by Fromm. The mighty Crimson Tide seemed one play from implosion, just as they were the previous January in the national title game. But the Bulldogs couldn't administer the knockout punch. They were close to a touchdown that would have made it 35–14 but had to settle for a 30-yard field goal and missed that. They let Alabama hang around, and Jalen Hurts came off the bench in relief of Tagovailoa to engineer a storybook 35–28 victory for Alabama. For much of the game, viewers wondered whether No. 1 Alabama would drop out of the CFP Top 4 by virtue of a blowout loss to the Bulldogs. The Tide's top ranking remained intact after another dramatic escape of Kirby Smart's team.

Clemson's coaches and players caught up on Alabama's remarkable win on a late-night bus ride back to Clemson from Charlotte. The popular takeaway from the Tide's victory was Hurts stepping up to be the hero while Tagovailoa ailed with the ankle injury. More scrutinizing observers might have recognized how close Alabama was to being blown out before Georgia failed to finish the job.

The Tigers motored along, seemingly content with their status as second fiddle to Alabama. Late the next morning, Clemson's bleary-eyed team gathered for a private pizza party inside the dining hall of the football operations facility. When the CFP pairings matched the No. 2 Tigers with No. 3 Notre Dame in the Cotton Bowl at Jerry World, the reaction was a relative golf clap compared to the full-throated celebration at Death Valley that had accompanied their entry to the CFP three years earlier. Over the five-year existence of the playoff, ten schools filled twenty spots. Seven of those schools experienced at least one five-loss season over that period from 2014 to 2018. Four of the schools had at least one losing season over those five years. Since losing to Georgia Tech late in 2014, Clemson had amassed a 56-4 record heading into the 2018 playoff.

In 2015, this was all new and wonderful and dream-like after a narrow victory over North Carolina in the ACC title game sealed Clemson's spot in the playoff. Swinney had promised a free pizza party at the stadium earlier that season if the Tigers made it to the CFP for the first time, and sure enough, the athletics department followed through in hosting a watch party at Death Valley as Clemson's semifinal pairing with Oklahoma was announced. In the three seasons since, everyone had grown used to winning big. Getting to the playoff is the holy grail to most of college football, but to Clemson, it had become the norm. So it was natural for everyone to greet the 2018 entry with something less than childlike excitement.

The head coach wasn't going to let it be a ho-hum affair, though. He pointed out that they were going to have a party even had they lost to Pittsburgh the night before, to celebrate a successful season and to reward a year's worth of hard work. Alabama, Georgia and Ohio State had better things to do than put on some silly watch party. Swinney had no problem ordering all the pizzas and then showing some of his dance moves. Clemson in the playoff had become the rule, but it was never going to be a mundane exercise for the man in charge.

Swinney even slipped on a cowboy hat during his live interview with ESPN's Rece Davis. Four straight ACC titles. Four straight CFP playoff trips. Four the win.

"We're just excited to be in the playoffs," he said. "This is what we've worked for all year long....Never been to Jerry World. Excited about it. Our guys are excited about it. We're going to paint Dallas orange."

CHAPTER 10

THE CAR RIDE

The caravan of buses awaited to whisk the team from Winston-Salem, away from the wreckage of one of the most reverberating defeats in Clemson football history. Away from that angry mob of orange-clad fans who wanted their coach fired before the buses reached the South Carolina state line. The final score was Wake Forest 45, Clemson 17. And it wasn't as close as those numbers indicated. Through three quarters, Clemson was down 45–0. To Wake. Wake Freaking Forest.

A first-year receivers coach named Dabo Swinney opted against the buses. He hopped in the car with his wife and three boys and spent the next four shellshocked hours with them instead. This was November 1, 2003. This was nine months after Swinney decided to leave an enormously promising career in commercial real estate because going to Clemson to get back into coaching just felt right. Joining Tommy Bowden was his calling. All the signs seemed to point to it, including this boy from Pelham, Alabama, seeing the sign for Pelham Road outside Greenville after he flew in for his interview.

Now, after the carnage that afternoon at Wake Forest, all the signs were pointing to Bowden, Swinney and everyone else being out of jobs. And quickly. Not just figurative signs. Actual signs, placed in Bowden's yard that night by spitting-mad fans telling him it was time to go. Five years later, another galling loss at Wake Forest would hasten Bowden's departure and put Swinney in the interim head-coach chair. Swinney managed to do enough to get the job for good, managed to hang on

Dabo and Kathleen Swinney celebrate in the 2018 national championship parade.

through some rocky times early in his tenure and then the juggernaut started to take shape. But in 2003, Swinney the first-year assistant coach was just trying to find a way to make it to the end of the season at this new home called Clemson.

Kathleen Swinney remembers that ride home from Wake Forest. She remembers the happy but nervous couple asking themselves: What have we gotten ourselves into? "We were a little concerned," she said. "We were thinking, 'OK, we'll just move on in December.'"

If Clemson doesn't pull off the unthinkable the next week by upending No. 3 Florida State 26–10, it's probably over for Bowden after five years. Former associate athletics director Bill D'Andrea basically confirmed as much to this writer in the fall of 2018. If the Tigers lose to the heavily favored Seminoles that 2003 night in Clemson, seven days after they were down 45–0 at Wake, the thirty-three-year-old Swinney has to update his résumé thusly:

—On Mike DuBose's fired staff in 2000. Not retained by successor.
—Left coaching for two seasons to sell commercial real estate.
—Lasted less than a year on Tommy Bowden's fired staff in 2003. Not retained by successor.

These are the type of stakes that would make most people shudder with fear in the moment. This is the type of what-if that makes most people wake up in cold sweats in hindsight. Dabo and Kathleen Swinney aren't like most people. Yes, they were kind of scared back in 2003. But they were mostly at ease with whatever happened, even as their third boy, Clay, was just two months old. Even as they were almost finished building a house, identical to the house in Birmingham they never got to live in because Dabo felt that calling in Clemson.

That week after Wake, as Bowden had to fight back tears at a press conference upon being asked if he believed he'd keep his job, the builder of the Swinneys' dream home approached with an awkward question. "I don't really know how to put this. But if things don't go well, I've got a lot of people that want to buy this house." Dabo's response: "I don't know if we're getting fired. But I know I'm moving into this house—for a couple of months anyway." They moved in and ended up living at 104 Sycamore for fourteen years before building a new palace in 2017, just a couple miles away. And now it seems like their forever home. Not the house itself. Clemson.

The story of Dabo's decade as Clemson's head coach is distinct mostly for the lengthy list of events and decisions that had to fall into place for him to get the interim job in the first place. Kathleen's view of that list is distinct for her lack of jaw-dropping amazement over all those pivotal, now-monumental junctures. "We just always felt like we were where we were supposed to be," she said.

It's remarkable to consider what had to happen (or not happen) to get them to Clemson. Following all those years as a coach and player at Alabama, Swinney had to clean out his office in Tuscaloosa after Dennis Franchione elected not to retain him. After Franchione left for Texas A&M, Swinney was overjoyed to get a call from Mike Price about joining his Crimson Tide staff. The deal was basically done for Swinney to coach tight ends. Then Price left to coach his old Washington State team one last time in the Rose Bowl. When he came back, Price called Swinney and told him he had a change of heart. He was going with a more seasoned coach for that position, Sparky Woods. The Price era at Alabama didn't last much longer, derailed by his dalliance at a strip club in Pensacola, Florida.

Through all that, Swinney was trying to get used to the real world while working for AIG Baker and crisscrossing the country leasing shopping centers. Watching Alabama games on TV was not a fun experience because Swinney believed he should be on that sideline doing what he did best. Not just the Alabama sideline. Any sideline. Kathleen will always remember Dabo pulling out of the driveway to start his first day at work at AIG Baker.

"As much of a blessing as it was for the eighteen months he was there, his whole career was starting new and it wasn't what he had always been doing. I was just so sad for him. I went inside and I just started crying. The phone rang, and I can't remember the player now. But one of our Alabama players' mom was calling just to talk to Dabo, to check in, to tell him how much she loved him. And it just made me cry even more. Because I'm like, 'He's supposed to be a coach.'"

Dabo was traveling a lot, and one trip brought him to Anderson. He came with the late Kevin Turner, former Alabama teammate and father of current Tiger Nolan Turner. They decided to take a side trip to Clemson to check out Death Valley. Dabo called Kathleen. "You're never going to believe where I am. Kevin and I just drove over here to Death Valley! To Clemson! It's so cool!"

Bowden was an assistant under Gene Stallings at Alabama for three years, the last in 1989, when Swinney earned a spot as a walk-on. So the Swinneys watched Bowden's teams often in 2001 and 2002. Then came the call from Bowden in February 2003, after Rick Stockstill left to become East Carolina's offensive coordinator. People told Bowden he was crazy for hiring a coach who'd been out of the business for so long. People told Swinney he was crazy for joining a staff that had finished 7-5 and been hammered 55–15 by Texas Tech in the Tangerine Bowl. Dabo came home one day and asked his wife, "What do you think about moving?' Kathleen thought he meant the move that was already planned for the next month, to their brand-new house in Birmingham. "No," Dabo said. "What do you think about moving to Clemson?"

Bowden and his staff ended up surviving that 2003 season, chasing away those vultures by winning their last four games by a combined score of 156–48. Three years later, Swinney had a chance to go back to Alabama. Rich Rodriguez had been offered the job and planned to accept. He wanted Swinney to come along, and his bags were packed. Rodriguez ended up backing out at the last instant. Ask Kathleen about this, and she doesn't make a big deal over it. This was when the Tigers were preparing for the Music City Bowl against Kentucky. Kathleen was busy being a mom.

"I remember having some doubt in my mind about that being something we should do," she said. "I think if you talk to any coach's wife, we just have to have a different mentality. Because there's so many ups and downs. You just have to stay planted where you are with your kids and you really can't think, 'Oh, we might be moving' or 'We might be fired.' You can't stop living. So I thought, 'Oh, OK. We'll cross that bridge if it really happens.'… It was Christmas. I had three little boys."

Around the same time, Dabo was up for the job at UAB and wanted it badly. He was set to interview and knew none of the other candidates would be as prepared. He had a full binder outlining his plan, and he'd already come up with slogans. "Blazer Nation!" Swinney recalled in the fall of 2018. "We were getting ready to build an empire."

Swinney was crushed when the AD called to cancel the interview. They hired Georgia assistant Neil Callaway. Swinney thought all he needed was to get in front of that AD, but it didn't happen. Around the same time, Nick Saban took the job that Rodriguez left. Saban called Swinney and offered him a huge raise and a title as passing-game coordinator. It didn't feel right because Swinney didn't know Saban at all and also because Swinney had six players committed who were about to sign with Clemson.

A year later after the Bowden-led Tigers lost the Atlantic Division title with a home loss to Boston College but then pulled out a last-second victory at South Carolina, Swinney was in Myrtle Beach recruiting. Bowden called him and told him to come back to Clemson. Arkansas was in hot pursuit of Bowden, and if Bowden took the job, he was taking Swinney with him.

"I remember being at the Central Rec at one of my boys' basketball games," Kathleen said. "Somebody came up to me and said, 'I hear y'all are going to Arkansas.' I'm like, 'What? No, I don't know anything. I'm just trying to do snack duty.' I didn't know any of that because Dabo hadn't called me yet."

Clemson's administration gave Bowden what he wanted, and the Arkansas plane left Oconee County Airport with empty seats. Less than a year later, Swinney suddenly became a major story when Bowden was out and he was in.

Ten years later—well, you know the story. And you should also know this: the happy couple doesn't sit around thinking about all those close calls, all the junctions and forks in the road that could have led them down a different path and away from the opportunity of a lifetime that came on October 13, 2008.

It's clear now to everyone that all those fateful decisions, whether by the Swinneys or others, were the right decisions. But Kathleen and Dabo don't need hindsight to make that conclusion; they've believed the whole time. All the way back to that quiet car ride from Wake Forest in 2003.

Dabo and Kathleen Swinney after beating Miami for the 2017 ACC championship.

"This is the tenth year since Dabo was named head coach, but this is our sixteenth year here," Kathleen said. "This is where I've raised my boys. This is home. I could really start to cry just talking about it. I have so many friends, so many memories. There's not a day that I drop the boys at Dabo's office where I don't go, 'Thank you, God.'"

CHAPTER 11

CLEMSON WORLD

The 2017 Sugar Bowl lurked in the minds of Clemson's coaches and players for much of the year, and the memory became even sharper as the Tigers turned their attention to the playoff. Though everyone stayed on message and preached "next game is the biggest game" all season, Alabama was always the elephant in the room. The Crimson Tide was the gold standard in college football, having won five national titles in nine years. Nick Saban's monster was the measuring stick, and for the 2018 Clemson team, it was the source of sour feelings based on the 24–6 humiliation in New Orleans the previous January.

The 2015 and 2016 offenses totaled 10 touchdowns against the Crimson Tide. The 2017 group didn't reach the end zone once over sixty miserable minutes in the Superdome. The Tigers totaled 188 yards that night, just 64 rushing, as a bloodthirsty Alabama defense physically overwhelmed Clemson at the line of scrimmage and elsewhere. Clemson was playing Notre Dame in this semifinal, not Alabama. But the lessons from the 2017 unraveling were important. The prolific offensive showings in 2015 and 2016 didn't come just from great passing from Deshaun Watson. The Tigers' receivers also supplied game-changing catches during those landmark moments.

The unforgettable images from the 2016 championship were of Mike Williams leaping high over an Alabama defender to snare a pass, Jordan Leggett twisting his body to grab another one and then Hunter Renfrow sealing it by cradling the ball in the right corner of the end zone. The defeat to the Crimson Tide a year later wasn't all on an inability to make the throws. The problem that night was more an inability to catch the throws. Deon Cain was wide open early on a third-and-long but dropped a perfect pass from Bryant. When Clemson finally had some momentum in the third quarter, Cain wasn't able to come down with the type of contested deep ball that Williams caught in his sleep. And then, after the Tide took a 17–6 lead, the game was sealed when a slant pass bounced off Cain's hands and into the grasp of Mack Wilson. The linebacker took the interception to the end zone, and Clemson was a long way from putting up 35 points and 511 yards against the Tide in Tampa.

Trevor Lawrence was the catalyst in making the offense lethal again. But the Tigers were also much different on the outside, where Tee Higgins and Justyn Ross were often uncoverable in 2018. At six-foot-four, these wideouts were more in the Williams mold. And defenses also had to worry about Renfrow, Amari Rodgers, Derion Kendrick, Trevion Thompson and Diondre Overton. Back during August camp, Swinney had said the receivers were going to be vastly improved over the 2017 group. And after thirteen games, they had more than backed up those words. Clemson ranked twenty-sixth nationally in passing plays of 20 yards or more with 50, twelfth in plays of 30 yards or more (28), fifth in plays of 40 yards or more (18) and seventh in plays of 50 or more (10). In fourteen games the previous season, Clemson had 40 passing plays of 20 yards or more, 18 of 30 or more, 11 of 40 or more and 6 of 50 or more. So this offense was pyrotechnic again through the air, which occupied defenders and opened space for the Tigers' highly successful running game.

Jeff Scott, who became receivers coach when Swinney took over as interim coach in 2008, spent December showing his receivers video clips of game-turning catches in recent years. Included were Williams's numerous grabs in 2016. There was nothing from the 2017 playoff.

In the ACC title game, Clemson's defense atoned for its night of busts and confusion against South Carolina. But outside observers were still wondering how the Tigers' secondary—and, more specifically, the safeties—would hold up in the playoff. Clemson defended the pass well for much of the season. It shut down Ryan Finley and the Wolfpack through the air. It locked in and locked down Syracuse late in that wild one. But the breakdowns in two games, Texas A&M and South Carolina, were hard to ignore. Clemson allowed a jarring 17 passing plays of 20 yards or more in those games alone.

"When we've had issues this year, it's not like people are just running by us and making these incredible plays and just beating us," Swinney said. "We've got guys running wide open because we don't line up right, we play

Notre Dame's safeties were no match for Justyn Ross.

poor leverage, we don't play with situational awareness. We really only had one game. Texas A&M was kind of an anomaly—second game, a lot of unknowns, a lot of things. And we got better. We played great all year. And then in the South Carolina game we didn't do a very good job. So it's important. It starts with your communication, making sure you know the call—it helps when you know the call—and communicating and lining up right, and formation recognition, and what comes off of it, and situational awareness, and alignments and splits, leverage, all those things. So we've got to do a great job of being dialed in so we can have good, clean execution. If guys make plays, they make plays. But let's make them earn it. Let's don't let guys be running wide open. Let's make sure we've got contested plays."

Clemson's defense remained confident, even when matched against an impressive group of receivers from Notre Dame and a quarterback who transformed the Irish offense earlier in the season. Ian Book was a major factor in Brian Kelly's team going through all twelve games unscathed. The Tigers were 12-point favorites in the Cotton Bowl, and that spread seemed high to most. But maybe the oddsmakers had paid attention to just how much of a nightmare Brent Venables can bring when he has extra time to prepare.

Dating to 2012, his first year at Clemson, Venables had put together a startling record of dominance in bowl games and CFP semifinals. The month of December allowed him time to cook up toxic recipes for opposing offenses. Starting with LSU in the Chick-fil-A Bowl, Clemson made life miserable for otherwise powerful rushing attacks.

Here are the following teams' rushing averages entering their bowl games against Clemson, followed by what they gained in the ground against the Tigers:

2012 LSU: 179.9 (99)
2013 Ohio State: 317 (193)
2014 Oklahoma: 268 (172)
2015 Oklahoma: 235 (67)
2016 Ohio State: 258.3 (88)
2017 Alabama: 259 (141)

So Clemson held six powerful rushing offenses to an average of 126.3 yards below what they rushed for against everyone else. Notre Dame came in averaging 190.5 rushing yards a game. The Irish piled up 365 yards on the ground against Florida State in their third-to-last game, and running back Dexter Williams was a dynamic back. But the Irish had yet to see anything like this Clemson defense.

On December 19, Clemson practiced for the last time on its campus, and Swinney gave everyone three full days off to go celebrate an early Christmas with family before the Tigers would depart for Dallas on December 23. This was intended to be a time to get away, decompress and recharge before devoting full focus to Notre Dame. But the day after he told his players goodbye, Swinney found his world rocked. The NCAA informed Clemson that three players—star defensive tackle Dexter Lawrence, freshman tight end Braden Galloway and reserve offensive lineman Zach Giella—had tested positive for a performance-enhancing drug called Ostarine. They faced a yearlong suspension under the NCAA's zero-tolerance policy, and Clemson scrambled to appeal.

For almost four days, Swinney kept this news from the team. A few high-ranking members of Clemson's athletics department knew, and so did university president Jim Clements and the school's legal counsel. But Swinney didn't even tell Venables until the team left for Dallas because he wanted his defensive coordinator and the rest of the team to savor their time off.

"Brent had no idea we weren't going to have Dexter until Sunday," Swinney said. "When we got on the plane, I told him. I didn't want to ruin anybody's Christmas. I found out Thursday. And I didn't tell anybody until Sunday because I knew what I was dealing with Thursday, Friday, Saturday. I didn't want to put that on my staff. I wanted them to just enjoy their time with their families and have a couple days off there."

The day after the team arrived in Dallas was Christmas Eve. Swinney, Hunter Renfrow and Kendall Joseph were scheduled to take part in a short press conference before the team's practice at AT&T Stadium. This writer had received a tip a few hours earlier that there was big news coming about a suspended player, possibly Lawrence. At the time, Swinney and Clemson still were not certain that they would make an announcement. Swinney did not announce anything during his opening statements, so this writer asked if everyone on the team was eligible, present and accounted for.

"We do have an issue that we're dealing with," Swinney responded. "And, you know, I think that the best thing is to just be transparent in that. This time of year, they obviously do—I mean, we test all year long. But on Thursday, Dan Radakovich was notified by the NCAA we had three guys that, you know, had a—there was an issue with their drug testing. And so been dealing with that since Thursday. And just—I think that the biggest thing is to make sure that, you know, everybody understands. Because I've had guys fail drug tests before. And usually, when you say a guy fails a drug test, people write their own stories. And they have their own innuendoes and their own narratives, and those type of things. And a lot of times, those things are accurate. But in this case, I think it's important, very important, that the message is accurate and that the truth is told because these are three great young men, three great young men, that I believe in and that I know, without a doubt, have not intentionally done anything to jeopardize their opportunity or this team. And I want to make that real clear before I even give you their names, because I know that's the story. But the letter that came from the NCAA said that these three young men had a sliver, a trace of some substance called Ostarine. I have no idea what Ostarine is. O-s-t-a-r-i-n-e. But I have become almost an expert in it in the last three days. There's plenty of stuff y'all can look at. But I would be willing to bet that there's a likelihood that, if they tested all of us right now, we might all or some of us have something in our system that we have no idea how it got there—a slither, a trace, a fraction. All right? This particular substance can come from anything. And these three players have no clue—in fact, they thought it was a joke when I called them. They have no clue how this has gotten in their system. It could come from hair products. It could come from a cream. It could come from protein. It could come from a product that you order or buy online that you think there's nothing wrong with it. It could be anything. Literally, it could be a drink—something in a drink. It literally could be anything, as I have come to learn. And, in fact, I think there's been forty or so athletes over the past year or so that have had to deal with this same exact thing. And several have later come back to be vindicated. They had no idea. Then they found out where it came from. So that's what we're in the process of doing. We're trying—we're going to do everything we can to figure out if it is in the system. Heck, I don't know. I mean, who's to say that it is there? I mean, that's what we're being told, but there's—they all will have legal representation, and there will be a process to go through to find out. But where we are right now is we got the three letters. And they have the—this trace. And so the next step is there's a B sample. And the B sample, they will test that. And we probably won't know until Wednesday or Thursday on that. So we're just kind of at the mercy of the process. And then there's an appeal after that, but that doesn't really help with this game. Maybe it helps for next week or, you know, next year, whatever. But that's what we're dealing with right now. But I want to be very clear that these guys, this is not street drugs. This is nothing like that. But the players are Braden Galloway, Zach Giella and Dexter Lawrence. Obviously, Dexter is a starter and a very, very significant player on our team. Even though Zach hasn't played as much and Braden is a freshman, they're still missing out on an opportunity that they have worked extremely hard for. And again, I don't know how—if it even is in their system—how it got there. But I do know that these three young men have not intentionally done anything. And there's, again, plenty of precedent where the same thing has happened across the country with other people. So, you know, there's a process in place. And we'll work through that. But from a team standpoint, we have to get our team ready to play football. We got to get our team ready to play our best four quarters of the season. That's our goal. So we have to prepare as if it's an injury and get the next guy ready. And that's exactly what we're going to do. So that's—I think it's just best, again, to be transparent and honest. Because I don't want there to be any speculation at all on what we're dealing with. That's exactly what we're dealing with. And I don't really know what else I can say about it other than I love all three of these guys. They're three special young people. And again, I know they've not intentionally done anything. And again, this is a hair of a trace of whatever this substance is. And so we'll deal with it accordingly, hope for the best, hope that the B sample will come back and they'll be cleared to play. But if not, we treat it as an injury. We've got to get ready to move forward. And our goal has not changed, just to play the best four quarters of the season."

This was a major bombshell to drop five days before the Cotton Bowl. Reporters scurried to learn more about a drug they'd never heard of, and so did fans. Social media was abuzz the day before Christmas. Here is an excerpt from the dispatch published by Tigerillustrated.com soon after Swinney's press conference:

The NCAA has a threshold with certain drugs, say marijuana. Meaning a player can have a small trace of that drug in his system but still not fail a drug test.

Not so with PEDs, for which the NCAA has a zero-tolerance policy. A mere trace, and you're done.

Everything we have gathered from trusted sources confirms Swinney's account that minuscule amounts of Ostarine came up in the tests of the aforementioned three players.

The bottom line right now: Even as Swinney and others hold out hope that a second sample will show no trace of the drug, the strong likelihood is that it will be similar to the first sample. That would mean the three players would not play in Saturday's Cotton Bowl against Notre Dame.

While the result from the second sample is expected Wednesday or Thursday, Clemson officials are devoting almost all of their efforts to an appeal that would allow the three players to be available for a possible national championship on Jan. 7, should the Tigers win Saturday.

Lawrence, of course, is the marquee name of this group. His absence from the playoff could be a very big deal, even though Clemson is lavished with gobs of talent on the defensive line even without him.

Galloway probably wasn't going to play much anyway. But the issue with him lies beyond this season; the NCAA suspension is one year, which would mean he'd miss the 2019 season barring successful appeal.

Our sources say Swinney informed the team of the news last night upon arrival to Dallas. Monday morning was spent trying to assess how to address the situation publicly. Swinney went the full-disclosure route, opting to give a comprehensive accounting of the situation after a question from Tigerillustrated.com during his pre-practice press conference.

Another possible route would've been to merely say the three players had been suspended for a violation of team rules, but the fallout from that could've been worse because it invites speculation about what the players did and suggests Swinney is trying to hide something.

It took considerable wrangling with the NCAA to sign off on the players making the trip. The basis was the remaining uncertainty surrounding the B sample. Clemson pushed for the three to make the trip so they could be a part of the team during the festivities during the run-up to the game.

We are told the staff is preparing as if the three will not be available. All three were present and dressed for practice today at AT&T Stadium, but the plan moving forward will have Albert Huggins getting a lot of work in Lawrence's place.

For Clemson, the NCAA's timing couldn't have been much worse. The news of the positive tests came right before the weekend, which is followed by Christmas Eve today and tomorrow's holiday. Thus the delay for the B-sample results until later this week.

On top of all this, Clemson is sifting through every piece of information possible to try to figure out how the small amount of Ostarine could've shown up. They're examining the finer print of hair products, acne cream, supplements, even the food that is served to the team in the dining hall of the football facility.

Three years ago, Swinney reacted swiftly and angrily when Deon Cain and others failed NCAA-mandated drug tests. He sent them home from Orange Bowl workouts and kicked Ammon Lakip off the team while saying Cain was one more strike from the same fate.

This case seems much different. Befuddlement seems to be the word of the past five days as the powers at Clemson have tried to sort through it all, with little success.

Before arriving in Dallas, the Tigers were all business and supremely focused. This news was a major distraction, though. Or at least it threatened to be. Two days later, several offensive and defensive players went in front of the media, and this was the dominant topic. Venables was grilled on it when he made his scheduled appearance. He said he had spent "zero time" thinking about it as he prepared for the Cotton Bowl. The NCAA's yearlong suspension meant that, barring appeal, Galloway and Giella would miss the 2019 season. Lawrence was widely considered likely to turn pro after his junior season, but he said he hadn't made up his mind at that point. So the suspension removed the slim chance Lawrence had of returning for his senior year.

"It's out of our hands," said defensive end Clelin Ferrell. "It's hard to even talk about because we know what type of people they are. It's not their fault. It wasn't intentional."

Outside the Clemson bubble, some followers of college football—particularly fans of rival schools—viewed this as an "Ah ha!" moment that revealed a nefarious secret to Clemson's success. That's just the nature of cynical partisan conjecture in today's social media world, regardless of the conviction on Clemson's part that no one did anything wrong.

"I know that we do everything ethically for the most part as a program," said Christian Wilkins. "We do a good job of just making sure we do the right things, and that's what Coach Swinney is big on and what he built the foundation of this program on is just doing things the right way and doing things differently. I think it would be foolish to say that, because I know I'm not doing anything and other people aren't doing anything intentional to help with their performance or anything like that. The reason for our success is from old-school hard work, grinding in the weight room, study film, practice hard, leadership and a good program."

The NCAA allowed Lawrence to make the trip and remain with the team. His presence meant a lot to his teammates even if he was out of uniform and helpless to do anything on the field. A day later, the Cotton Bowl held its official media day. The College Football Playoff sought to make this an event similar to the Super Bowl's annual media-day circus, so each team is mandated to make everyone on the team available for interviews—players, coaches, support staffers, everyone. It was just assumed by the media that Lawrence would not be present for this event, which took place on the field at AT&T Stadium. But before Clemson arrived, there was his name on a placard sitting on a table. Sure enough, the big guy showed to face the questions and the white-hot glare of scrutiny. Lawrence, Galloway and Giella weren't required to go. "Coach left it up to them and said, 'We'll support you either way,'" said Ross Taylor, the football communications director. "Dexter was adamant about participating and speaking for himself."

On the artificial turf, facing an inquisition about artificial strength, Lawrence seemed real. "I just wanted to come because I consider myself a leader and I just wanted guys to know I've got their back just like they've got mine." He said he was "mind-boggled" when Swinney called with the news. "I was in shock. I was looking at my phone like, 'Are you crazy? What is wrong with you for asking me something like that?' Next thing you know he tells me I've tested positive for something I've never heard of or know where to get it." Lawrence said he sticks to a strict routine on what he puts into his body.

"I'm not the type of guy to do a selfish act like that. I have too much pride. I love this team and I love my family too much to even think about putting a substance like that in my body. I don't know where it came from. I don't know how it got there. I was raised different. If I did do it, I'd own up to it. All I can say is I honestly don't know where it came from or how it got here. It's just there. There's nothing I can really do about it."

It's hard to know whether Lawrence's absence galvanized the team or whether the Tigers were just that much better than Notre Dame to begin with. With talented veteran backup Albert Huggins taking Lawrence's place, Clemson was its typical disruptive self on the defensive front. The first quarter ended at 3–3 as the offense tried to get comfortable. But it wouldn't be long before Trevor Lawrence and his receivers started supplying precisely the type of downfield plays that were in such short supply the previous year against Alabama. Lawrence found Justyn Ross for a 52-yard touchdown strike down the right sideline less than three minutes into the second quarter. Clemson was moving the ball now, and after a missed field goal on the next possession, Lawrence got to work again. Lawrence had already connected with Ross for 35 yards on third-and-7 on the previous drive to put Clemson in scoring position, but a holding call set the offense back and led to the missed field goal. A false-start penalty on the next possession turned a third-and-9 into a third-and-14 from Notre Dame's 42. Ross was in the slot and matched up against a safety. He made easy work of getting by him, and when he broke open, the ball was already in the air. The perfect pass caught him in stride, and the 42-yard touchdown put the Irish in a 17–3 hole with 1:44 left in the half.

Jeff Scott, the receivers coach, said Ross was sensational during bowl practices. He saw a big night coming from the freshman from Alabama. "I told his mama before the game and I told him: I have a feeling tonight is going to be a coming-out night for you."

Notre Dame couldn't do anything, and Clemson got the ball back at its 20-yard line with 48 seconds on the clock and one timeout left. The Tigers smelled blood and sensed an opportunity to leave no doubt right here before halftime. Lawrence hit Amari Rodgers for a first down to get things going. Then Renfrow faked the safety out of his shoes on a route and Lawrence hit him down the middle for 32 yards. Notre Dame's star defensive lineman Jerry Tillery took a shot at Lawrence well after he threw it, drawing a personal-

Even without Dexter Lawrence, the Tigers' defensive line controlled the line of scrimmage against Notre Dame.

foul penalty that tacked on 15 more yards. Suddenly, Clemson was 19 yards from another touchdown.

With nine seconds on the clock, Clemson used its last timeout to settle on a play. Higgins was split to the right side, covered man-to-man by backup cornerback Donte Vaughn with a safety lurking over the top. At the snap, the safety rolled toward the middle of the field. That left Higgins one-on-one. Lawrence recognized it and threw it up. Vaughn had his back turned as he tried to keep up with Higgins. Vaughn raised his left arm and tipped the ball directly to the right hand of Higgins, who somehow managed to secure it while getting a foot in bounds in the back of the end zone. Four plays, 80 yards, touchdown.

In a mere 238 seconds, Clemson ran 12 plays that totaled 165 yards and produced two touchdowns to put the Irish in a 23–3 halftime hole. In the second quarter alone, Lawrence passed for 229 yards and three touchdowns while completing 13 of 15 passes. He made observers wonder if he'd be the first pick in the NFL draft, like, right now. "Every ball he throws is perfect," Ross said of Lawrence. "You have to try to drop his ball."

The absence of one Lawrence didn't really mean anything. The presence of another Lawrence meant everything. Well, almost everything. Because

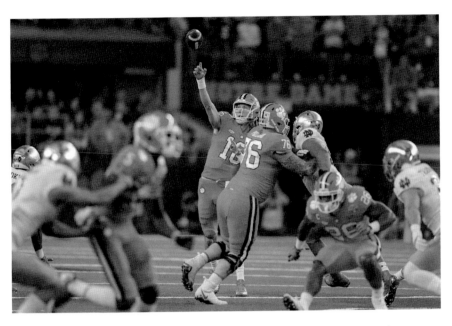

Trevor Lawrence and his receivers abused Notre Dame's secondary in the second quarter.

the Tigers were positively electric at receiver. And Venables's defense did the same old throttling of an opposing offense by asphyxiating the Irish running game and frazzling Book. Notre Dame finished with 88 rushing yards, more than 100 less than its average coming in. The second half was basically a formality, the same script as so many other Clemson games in 2018. The elevated stage and the tradition-rich opponent made no difference.

In the locker room after the game, national reporters asked coaches and players if Lawrence's effortless dismantling of Notre Dame's defense was a surprise. People spent much of the season waiting for this nineteen-year-old to make some freshman mistakes. They were going to have to wait at least another week.

"This is not a surprise," Scott said. "I told our guys before the game when we were talking to our offense: 'Hey, we've got one of the best quarterbacks in the country, and I can't wait to watch him play on this stage.' It was not a surprise to any of us. We've been able to see this since he got there in January. The exciting part for us is he's only going to get better."

As Clemson was going through its postgame media interviews and then walking to the buses, Alabama was mounting a 28–0 assault in the first

Travis Etienne closes the deal for Clemson in the third quarter of the Cotton Bowl.

Trevor Lawrence and ESPN's Tom Rinaldi after the Cotton Bowl.

half of the Orange Bowl against Oklahoma. The Crimson Tide was up 31–10 at halftime, and national media voices were quick to present this as confirmation that Alabama was without peer in 2018. The Sooners rallied and found holes in Alabama's defense. Oklahoma's defense couldn't come up with a stop, and the Tide won 45–34. When Clemson's coaches watched the film of Kyler Murray throwing for 308 yards and two touchdowns, they saw some vulnerability in Alabama's defense that excited them.

But first things first: after the bitter taste of losing in the semifinal in 2017, the Tigers were back in the national championship game for the third time in four years. They'd turned Jerry World into Clemson World. The celebration did not come close to matching the unbridled joy that accompanied Clemson's semifinal win over Oklahoma in 2015, when Clemson got to the championship game for the first time. The reaction this time was more businesslike, as if they planned to be there all along. As if they planned to do what almost no one on the outside expected.

After the game, Ferrell removed his shoulder pads and his undershirt revealed a message scrawled in Sharpie: "This for big Dex."

CHAPTER 12

THE PARKING SPACE

H e'd been the head coach for the better part of three days, but he couldn't bring himself to move to the head coach's office. The thought of putting himself into the chair Tommy Bowden occupied for nine-plus years just felt weird and awkward.

But finally, Dabo Swinney decided it was time. Life as an assistant coach in the McFadden Building was always sort of distracting, because the doors were wide open and anyone and everyone could stroll right through. It was a totally normal occurrence for fans and media to pop their heads into the offices to chat, as if the coaches were just sitting around waiting to talk about stuff. Swinney thought the building was kind of like a fishbowl, with windows wrapped around the whole thing to give passersby an up-close view of the coaches' world.

So now he was suddenly the big fish, as of late Monday morning on October 13, 2008. For the next forty-eight-plus hours, he tried to get stuff done in the small office he'd occupied since he arrived in the spring of 2003, with the view of Littlejohn Coliseum across Perimeter Road and Death Valley even farther back to the right behind a row of trees. "I finally realized I couldn't get anything done," Swinney recalled. "Because it was a constant thoroughfare."

After practice on Wednesday evening, Swinney decided to pack up some boxes and make the move over to the vacant corner office on the other side of McFadden, overlooking the baseball stadium. Bowden's office had a sliding-glass door that allowed quick and easy access to and from his

Dabo Swinney, back at the McFadden Building in October 2018—ten years after he became the head coach in the same building. *By Larry Williams.*

parking spot five steps away. Swinney was given the keys to that door and thought it was cool.

Thursday morning arrived, and he drove to work in the dark ready to begin his first day in the head man's office. But he was an emotional wreck. The almost total lack of sleep over the week to that point probably had something to do with it. Monday, Tuesday and Wednesday were just straight adrenaline and emotion, starting with the moment Terry Don Phillips surprised him by telling him he wasn't just some holdover coach keeping things together until Phillips found the right guy for the job. The AD told him not to act like an interim coach, to act like a head coach in charge of a program. No guarantees, but it was clear Phillips thought Swinney had exactly what this rollercoaster program needed.

So this was a startling and transforming revelation. Swinney actually had a shot at this thing, and for three days it was one hundred miles an hour with positive energy and a vapor trail of All-In. But even one of the most optimistic humans on the planet isn't immune to insecurities and low moments, and Swinney was starting to feel like maybe it was all too much as he drove his Ford Explorer down Highway 93, past the Esso Club and took a left on Perimeter. He was the first one into the parking lot that morning.

"I mean, it's getting real now," he said. "I've been through Monday, Tuesday and Wednesday and I've had very little sleep. I always kind of pray when I come in to work anyway. And I was just emotional that Thursday morning. I was a little overwhelmed. A lot of it was I was just tired. And I think with any normal person there's a little fear. It's like, 'Man. This is for real.'"

With the benefit of hindsight, it's easy to view everything as being meant to be. As if everything just fell into place in a nice and tidy way, following what has become a classic movie script. But nothing was nice and tidy in the moment. Don't let the mountain of wins, the two national titles and four consecutive playoff appearances fool you into thinking that 4-2 record over the last six games under Swinney in 2008 wasn't a feat.

You have to remember how much of a mess that team was. Ranked in the Top 10 entering the season, they were 3-3, and it was the worst kind of 3-3 you can imagine; two of those wins were over The Citadel and South Carolina State. Swinney had fired Rob Spence. His new receivers coach was Jeff Scott, who'd previously been a graduate assistant on defense. Swinney didn't really get along with his defensive coordinator, Vic Koenning, who probably thought he was better qualified than Swinney to be the head coach. He was trying to unite a team that had just lost its coach. And, oh by the way, a good Georgia Tech team was visiting in two days. "I was distracted by things that don't matter, people saying all kind of stuff," Swinney said. "Just stuff."

For five years, Swinney always parked on the side of the McFadden parking lot facing Perimeter Road. He was headed to that same spot per his routine when he remembered there was a vacant space right next to the corner office. Bowden's spot. So Swinney wheeled around and pointed the Explorer to that space.

"As I pull in, my lights hit this curb," Swinney said last fall, standing at that precise spot.

He immediately hit the brakes when his eyes narrowed and he saw the number on the curb. That would be 88, the number he wore at Alabama. "I stopped right there. And I just started crying."

He called his wife and said, "You're not going to believe this." Earlier in the week, minutes after Phillips told the staff that Swinney was the interim guy, Swinney had called Kathleen and told her they'd been fired. "And it

In 2008, Dabo Swinney broke down crying when he saw that his new parking space featured the same number he wore at Alabama. *By Larry Williams.*

gets worse: I'm the interim," he told her on the way to another meeting with Phillips.

At that moment, minutes after learning Bowden was out and he was the guy, Swinney took no comfort in knowing he was in charge. He'd been at Alabama in 2000, the year Mike DuBose and his fired staff finished out the season knowing they were gone. That was an awful experience. And that's exactly what was in Swinney's mind as he walked to Phillips's office that day, giving his wife a quick update and hearing her sobbing into his cellphone. They were embarking on seven weeks of hell, and then they were going to be moving somewhere else.

"There just really wasn't much positive in my mind. I'm worried about my family, where I'm going to be moving. I'm worried about my players, the kids I've got recruited."

But then everything changed when Swinney walked into Phillips's office. The AD began the conversation by saying, "I want you to know I've watched you five and a half years. And I want you to know I think you're ready for this job."

Swinney was stunned. Phillips continued: "Here's what I want you to do: For the next seven weeks, I don't want you to be the interim head coach. I want you to be the head coach. I want you to think like you're the head coach. I want you to do whatever you think you need to do to fix us. Do it, and you've got my full support. If you feel like you've got to fire the whole staff, you've got my full support. I've watched you in the community. I've watched your relationships with your players. I've watched how you coach on the field. I've watched you in recruiting. I've watched how you manage yourself. Dabo, I really believe you're what we need here. Now I'm also going to tell you this: I'm going to hire the best coach for Clemson. I'm going to do a national search and I'm going to interview people. But what I want you to know is I would love to see you get this job."

Those words changed everything. Before he returned to the chaos of the football offices, Swinney locked himself in a small break room near Phillips's office and spent forty-five minutes writing every thought that came to mind in a notebook.

"All of a sudden I went from one emotion to adrenaline," he said. "I was inspired. I was so motivated: 'Man, I've got a shot!' I mean it was

Dabo Swinney back at his old parking spot in October 2018. *By Larry Williams.*

just a complete extreme stream of emotions, back and forth. I just started writing stuff down. It was all over the place. Practice thoughts, staff thoughts, recruiting thoughts, fan thoughts, team thoughts...just a flood of emotion."

Three days later probably felt like three months later, but the adrenaline had worn off, and now Swinney needed another lift as he pulled in to his new parking space before the sun came up. He needed some sort of sign to help him take the next step, out of his car and through that sliding-glass door and into the corner office that was now his.

At some point thereafter, Swinney pulled open Bowden's top desk drawer and grabbed a pen. He wrote his first name in ink and retraced it several times, then underlined it. Whether he succeeded or not, he was going to leave his mark. Current athletics director Dan Radakovich now occupies the same desk, and the name is still at the bottom of that top drawer.

"I always tell people that I think God winks at you sometimes," Swinney said, standing beside spot no. 88. "It was definitely a moment in my life where I felt God just kind of put his arm around me and said, 'Hey look, I've got you right where I want you. Don't have any fear. Don't have any doubt.

In 2008, Dabo Swinney scrawled his name into a drawer of his new desk when he became interim head coach. Athletics director Dan Radakovich now uses the same desk. *By Larry Williams.*

125

You've prepared for this. But more importantly, I've got your back.' And it was just this moment of peace."

On Monday, he walked out of Phillips's office empowered by his boss. On Thursday, he walked into the head coach's office—his office—empowered by a higher power.

"From that point forward, I had this total peace. I didn't know how it was going to work out, but I didn't really care anymore. I was just focused on what I needed to do. And I knew that God was ordering my steps."

CHAPTER 13

CLEMSON TIDE

The modern-day culture of following sports makes us eager to crown something that is about to happen, is happening or has just happened as "the best ever." There is at least one "Game of the Century" per season in college football. In 2003, Oklahoma went on a scorched-earth tour through the regular season, and some observers wondered if they were the best team ever. Then Kansas State upended the Sooners 35–7 in the Big 12 championship game, and LSU spanked them in the BCS title game. The "best ever" label was quickly forgotten, discarded to a waste bin full of similar labels for other teams. In 2011, people were calling Alabama the best team ever. And then LSU went to Tuscaloosa and upset the Crimson Tide 9–6. Then the Bayou Bengals were in that same discussion, until they couldn't move the ball an inch against Alabama in the BCS title game.

But it's not all breathless, baseless hyperbole. Not when the most dominant run in college football history is in progress. From 2009 to 2017, Nick Saban won five national titles at Alabama. And he was tantalizingly close to a sixth before Deshaun Watson and Clemson went down the field and scored with one second left in Tampa. So it was perfectly reasonable to wonder if certain Alabama teams were the greatest ever assembled. The Tide were stockpiling five-star recruits, and they had lapped the rest of the SEC as schools fired coaches left and right while bringing in former Saban assistants to try to acquire some of his secret sauce. And from the start of the 2018 season, Alabama had added a whole new dimension to its arsenal: an

Dabo Swinney, intense during warm-ups before the national championship.

aggressive, attacking offense loaded with talent and catalyzed by sophomore quarterback Tua Tagovailoa.

Previously, Saban had adapted his ground-and-pound offensive ways to make the Tide more modern in an era of spread sets and up-tempo pace. But even as the presence of Jalen Hurts in 2016 and 2017 brought more run-pass options and more playmaking from the quarterback position, Alabama's offense was still based in minimizing risk and leaning on a defense that overwhelmed most everyone.

From the moment Tagovailoa was inserted in the 2017 CFP title game with Alabama facing a 13–0 halftime deficit, everything changed. Saban was ready to play his backup against Clemson in the semifinal a week earlier if his offense continued to struggle, but he didn't need to because the Tigers' offense couldn't do much of anything that night in the Superdome.

Now, suddenly, Alabama's offense was at the forefront of an offensive revolution that had taken hold in not just college football but the NFL too. The Tide was stretching the field horizontally and vertically as Tagovailoa hit ultra-talented receivers in perfect stride on deep balls. Alabama still had an embarrassment of riches at running back and a big physical offensive line to smash people with the run when defenses attempted to keep the deep ball from killing them. It was a stunning sight to behold. Two weeks after Alabama torched Louisville 51–14 in its opener, the Crimson Tide went to Mississippi and fell behind 7–0 early on a deep ball. All Tagovailoa and Alabama did from there was score 62 unanswered points and win by 55.

Suddenly, Alabama was must-see TV for the average college football fan. The Tide's method had somehow mutated from methodical suffocation via brute force to a high-flying aerial show that knocked out teams early. Over its 6-0 start, Alabama outscored the opposition 124–21 in the first quarter. In the seventh game against Missouri, it felt like a moral victory for the Tigers to be within 13–10 of the Tide after fifteen minutes. (Bama reeled off 17 points in the second quarter to make things feel normal again.)

After a 58–21 flushing of Tennessee in Knoxville, Alabama had an off week to prepare for its biggest test: a trip to Baton Rouge to face a No. 4 LSU team that had given Alabama some trouble the year before. But the Tide proceeded to embark on a familiar soul-crushing exhibition of superiority in a 29–0 victory that felt worse than the final score indicated. Alabama rolled up 576 yards of total offense, and Tagovailoa had no problem slicing up a decorated LSU secondary while throwing for 295 yards. Many in the national media, ever quick to make ironclad conclusions, rendered a final judgment on the 2018 season three days into November: the path was clear for Saban to bring home a sixth national title in ten years, and Tagovailoa was a lock for the Heisman.

Meanwhile, Clemson had shifted into a higher gear and was destroying people too. It was totally fair to wonder about the Tigers' credentials when they were trying to find their way in September amid the juggling of two quarterbacks. But then they massacred four consecutive opponents (Wake Forest, N.C. State, Florida State, Louisville) by a combined score of 240–36. Their offense with Trevor Lawrence at the controls was terrifying for a lot of the same reasons Alabama was terrifying with the Hawaiian sensation at quarterback. And it looked as if Clemson's defense was better than Alabama's, Brent Venables's best yet thanks in large part to a defensive line that lived in opponents' backfields.

But proceeding through November and early December, there was never much hint of "best ever" talk associated with Clemson. It never crossed the mind of pundits or anyone on the outside of the Tigers' football program for two reasons: 1) Alabama was still supposedly a cut above; and 2) Clemson's annihilation of opponents wasn't as impressive because those opponents were from a conference that wasn't any good.

Trevor Lawrence and Clelin Ferrell, minutes before kickoff in the national championship.

So this was the backdrop that accompanied the meeting of two 14-0 teams in the CFP title game. Clemson was viewed as capable of not just playing with the Tide but beating them. Three years earlier, plenty of people wondered whether the Tigers could stay on the same field as Alabama. But perceptions were much different now, evidenced not just by the opening line of 6.5 points in favor of what was being called the best team in history, but also by much of the gambling action going in Clemson's favor to trim the spread even more as the week progressed.

A fourth consecutive meeting between the Tide and Tigers drew some complaints from fans and media who said the same thing every year was getting stale. But for college football connoisseurs, this was a matchup for the ages between two monsters that had established clear separation from the rest of the field.

Taking away their head-to-head matchups from 2015 to 2017, Alabama and Clemson had combined to win 106 of their previous 110 games. The Tide had beaten its 2018 opponents by an average of 31.5 points per game. The Tigers' margin was 31.4. Alabama ranked first nationally in offensive efficiency and second in defensive efficiency. Clemson ranked fourth in the former and first in the latter.

Both teams had gobs of future NFL talent, and on both offenses most of it consisted of freshmen and sophomores. The 2015 and 2016 title games between the two were two of the best in college football history. This matchup looked like it could produce an even more entertaining game, as difficult as that sounded given that Clemson's 2016 title was won with a second on the clock.

ESPN's Brad Edwards told a Tuscaloosa radio station that this was a matchup for the ages: "This isn't just another Bama-Clemson game. This isn't just another matchup of two undefeated teams for the national championship. This is one of the greatest single-game matchups we've ever seen in college football history."

Before Clemson left for Santa Clara, it learned Dexter Lawrence wouldn't be available for the final game either. The NCAA denied Clemson's appeal to have him reinstated but allowed him to make the trip and watch the Tigers try to contain Alabama's prolific offense. His absence wasn't a big deal against Notre Dame, but outsiders viewed it as a very big deal against Alabama.

The two main concerns about Clemson were protecting Trevor Lawrence, and its safeties covering Alabama's dynamic and explosive inside receivers. A year earlier, the Tide's defensive line abused the Tigers' offensive line in the Sugar Bowl. Alabama returned everyone but Da'Ron Payne, who wreaked havoc that night in New Orleans. But in Payne's spot was Quinnen Williams, regarded as the top defensive lineman in college football. Williams was almost impossible to block all season and even picked up Heisman votes.

"It's insane," Clemson offensive lineman John Simpson said of Williams. "I don't know what they feed those guys, but he became an animal."

Clemson had done an exemplary job of protecting Lawrence for much of the season. But this was a different animal. This was Alabama, which made Kelly Bryant's night a living hell a year earlier. In 2015 and 2016, Watson's legs were as essential as his arm in going blow-for-blow with Alabama. Now the Tigers had a quarterback with generational arm talent, but he was not the jitterbug that was thought essential in escaping Alabama's pressure and extending drives.

Publicly, Clemson's coaches lavished Alabama with the praise and adulation befitting a colossus that was going for its sixth title since 2009. Swinney said the two teams were mirror images. Venables said Alabama was like "Darth Vader" and made it sound like stopping the Tide's offense was an impossible task. He pointed out that as good as Clemson's defense was, Alabama had only offered scholarships to a handful of the players on the Tigers' defensive roster. He was asked how preparing for this offense on a week's notice compared to preparing for a much different Alabama offense a year earlier with almost a month to get ready.

"I think it's probably easier because you just don't have as many grueling hours of torture," he said. "Against these guys, it's frightening. Their ability to execute, their explosiveness. They get the ball to their skills, whether it's 8 or 11 or 17, and they've got this guy 4 and this guy 82 or 22 or 34 or 13 or 2. It's sickening. But our guys are excited about the challenge. We are too, to see where we match up. It's a great, great challenge for us. Easily the best challenge, probably the best group we've seen as an offense since I've been at Clemson."

It wasn't crazy to see this as a bad matchup for Clemson's defense. The Tigers gave up explosive passing plays by the bushel against South Carolina and Texas A&M, and now they were facing the most explosive offense in the country. Alabama's top five receivers were averaging more than 16 yards per catch. In 2017, the Tide had 42 passing plays of 20 yards or more in 14 games. At the same point in 2018, they had 78 passing plays of 20-plus yards.

Clemson's defensive staff was quietly optimistic, though. Even without Dexter Lawrence, there was no reason for them to think their defensive line wouldn't disrupt as it had all year. Also, Tagovailoa had regressed some over his last six games, throwing four interceptions after tossing zero over his first eight. He was injured early in the SEC title game against Georgia, but he still made two poor decisions in throwing interceptions that the Bulldogs picked off at the goal line. On November 10, Mississippi State's defensive line sped him up and made him uncomfortable. At one point, he threw an interception directly into the arms of an MSU defender on an intermediate throw.

Alabama's offense was indeed redefined as one that could strike at any time and score points in bunches. It was authentically one of the biggest challenges of Venables's coaching career. But he and his staff saw a vulnerability in this new offensive style. More aggression meant more to defend, yes. But it also meant more chances for the ball to be in danger. Once Tagovailoa's first read was covered, he tended to be careless with the ball. In addition, he was loose with the ball in the pocket as he juked and jived around defenders to buy more time to throw. This was the mother of all tasks for Venables and his staff. But Tagovailoa, who finished second in the Heisman voting after his forgettable showing against Georgia, hadn't seen anything like what they were about to throw at him.

On the other side of the ball, Clemson's offensive coaches were brimming with confidence and doing a great job of hiding it when the media were around. One of the only clues came on media day, when this reporter was

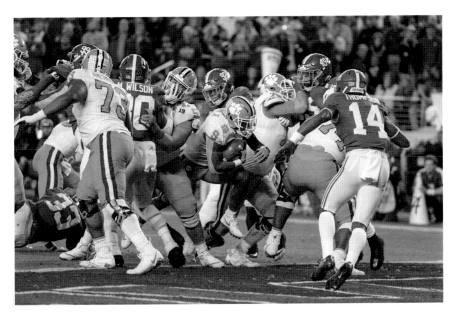

Travis Etienne bulls through for a touchdown against Alabama.

speaking with co–offensive coordinator Jeff Scott. Asked if Bama corners Patrick Surtain and Saivion Smith were the best corners Clemson had faced in 2018, Scott initially gave a smirk that spoke volumes. Then he offered the typical coach-speak and praised them. In truth, Scott and the rest of the offensive staff thought the corners at Notre Dame and Pittsburgh were better. So confident was Scott that his receivers could abuse the Crimson Tide's secondary, he told people close to him that Clemson was winning this game by double digits. A year earlier, Tee Higgins was a freshman and played just four snaps against Alabama after aggravating an ankle injury. Justyn Ross was still in high school in Phenix City, Alabama, likely headed to Clemson but still being chased hard by Alabama and Auburn. After suffering from the loss of Mike Williams in 2017, the Tigers were back to owning one-on-one matchups at receiver.

"Eleven months ago, we were coming off a very disappointing loss to Alabama," Scott said. "We were not able to make the plays down the field that we did the year before with Mike Williams. That was a big selling point that we told Ross. We said, 'Hey, you can help us beat Bama because we need a big receiver like you to make those plays. We could be there next year, and you as a freshman could be one of the real difference-makers in that game.'"

The offensive line still had to protect, though, because Lawrence's golden arm could do no good if he was not upright. The Tigers struggled to run the ball consistently against Notre Dame in the first half, and the Irish sacked Lawrence three times. Behind closed doors, this group of linemen and coach Robbie Caldwell were seething about the stuff being said in the media. They were called "pedestrian." A rampage by Quinnen Williams seemed a given, and aside from that, Clemson was going to have a hard time blocking the guys that owned the line of scrimmage a year before. They were sick of being regarded as the "weak link." Sick of hearing about how much Alabama ground them into the artificial turf in New Orleans. Sick of hearing about how an otherwise great season would ultimately be defined by their inability to hold up against mighty Alabama.

In the last twenty-four hours of airtime that had to be filled before kickoff at Levi's Stadium, the common opinion seemed to be this: Bama-Clemson Part 4 looked like another war, similar to 2015 and 2016. And if it was a blowout, the Crimson Tide would be the team administering it. Either Clemson was going to pull out a dramatic victory and be on even footing with Alabama, or the Crimson Tide was going to strengthen its death grip on the rest of college football. These were the only two possibilities, almost as if it was engraved in stone.

The thought of a Clemson romp occurred to almost no one, and for good reason: because no one had ever done such a thing to Saban's killing machine. During Alabama's title run from 2009 to 2017, the Tide had lost 12 total games. Just 3 of those losses were by double digits, and the largest margins were to South Carolina in 2010 (35–21) and Oklahoma in 2013 (45–31). And both of those games got away from the Tide in the final fifteen minutes. Against the Gamecocks, Alabama was within 28–21 with eight minutes left in the game. Against the Sooners, the Tide were down 31–24 entering the fourth quarter.

In other words, Alabama had never been humiliated like the rest of college football gets humiliated on occasion. Even Swinney's towering program is not that far removed from a couple of curb-stompings—51–14 to Florida State in 2013 and 70–33 to West Virginia two years earlier.

During one period years ago, Saban's dynasty was thought to have cracks in the foundation. The world was becoming different, largely because of offensive innovation. Saban was used to loading up on defensive players who were bigger and stronger at all three levels and overwhelming opposing offenses at the point of attack. This makes perfect sense if you're playing a one-dimensional, conventional LSU team for the national title in 2011 and

Tee Higgins gets free early on third-and-long for a long gain that set up a touchdown after Alabama scored.

winning 21–0 to avenge a 9–6 loss during the regular season. Or a Notre Dame team that is completely overmatched in the 2012 BCS title game a year later.

But a common thread emerged in the rare conquests of Saban's machine: exceptional playmaking at quarterback, starting with Cam Newton in 2010 and continuing with Johnny Manziel in 2012 and then extending to Nick Marshall (Auburn) and Trevor Knight (Oklahoma) in 2013. A year later, Ohio State's Cardale Jones picked apart Saban's defense in the semifinal of the inaugural playoff. Stretching Alabama horizontally and vertically, the Buckeyes rushed for 281 yards and passed for 256 in a 42–35 victory on the way to a national championship.

In Alabama's third game of 2015, Chad Kelly and Mississippi went to Tuscaloosa and sliced up the Tide's defense in a 43–37 upset. That was the moment plenty of observers pronounced last rites to Saban's dynasty. But in reality, he had already adapted by going smaller on defense to compensate for all the spread formations. His safeties were basically cornerbacks. His linebackers were smaller, and he often used a fifth defensive back. His defensive linemen were quicker and more agile, like linebackers. On offense, Saban began to go with the styles that were hurting him most on defense. He had hired Lane Kiffin to modernize the offense, using dual-threat capabilities at quarterback, spreading the field horizontally and using tempo.

The loss to Mississippi handed Alabama its fifth loss in 19 games dating to the end of 2013. Just when the pundits were saying Saban's model had grown creaky and vulnerable, the Tide commenced a run that made a mockery of those assessments. They won 12 straight that year, including a 45–40 triumph over Clemson for the national championship. They won 14 straight the next year before losing to the Tigers in Tampa. Then 13-1 and a championship in 2017, followed by the 14-0 record they took to Santa Clara.

But that ruthless reassertion of supremacy—2 losses in 55 games, after 5 losses in 19 games—did make it easy to gloss over some recent moments when the Tide was wobbly. In 2017, Alabama was close to not making the CFP field after its offense was a mess in a 26–14 loss at Auburn. And then in that year's title game, the Tide seemed one Georgia score from implosion before Tagovailoa led the comeback from deficits of 13–0 and 20–7.

In the 2018 SEC championship, Georgia was taking it to Alabama on both sides of the ball. The Tide was down 28–14 in the third quarter, and the Bulldogs were moving down the field for another score. Reach the end zone there, or even kick a field goal, and maybe Alabama comes unglued

Alabama tight end Irv Smith Jr. struggles to hold up against Clelin Ferrell.

136

and Georgia rolls to a dominating win. But the Bulldogs' drive stalled short of the end zone, and then they missed a 30-yard field goal. They were close to leaving no doubt, but they left the door open instead.

Round 4 was played as far away as possible from college football's heartland as the CFP tried to spread interest in the game across the country. The game could have been played in London and there wouldn't have been less local buzz as people in the San Francisco area wondered what was going on with all this orange and crimson on their streets. The lack of casual interest sparked predictions of wide swaths of empty seats at Levi's Stadium, home of the San Francisco 49ers. But large numbers of Clemson and Alabama fans managed to get there despite exorbitant prices on flights and hotels, and with few empty seats, the matchup had a fitting atmosphere with an announced attendance of 72,360.

Interviews with coaches seconds before kickoff seldom provide much profound insight, but in this instance, the brief conversations presented some foreshadowing. Swinney, privately convinced he had the better team, told ESPN's Tom Rinaldi that his final instructions to his players were: "Dominate this moment. That's what it's all about." Saban, who entered the game unable to shake the feeling that his defensive backs were going to have a hard time covering Clemson's receivers, offered this to Maria Taylor when asked about the greatest challenge of defending Lawrence: "They've got really good outside players. And the real key to the game to me is how we manage and control and keep those guys cut off."

Clemson had the ball first and continued its trend of slow starts with a three-and-out. Alabama took over at its 21, and it was business as usual for Tagovailoa, who hit tight end Irv Smith for 8 yards and then fired a perfect strike to DeVonta Smith for 12 yards and a first down.

Earlier in the day, former Florida quarterback Tim Tebow appeared on ESPN and shared his account of what it was like to face a defense coached by Venables. In 2008, Florida was chasing its second national title in three years. Alabama would surpass the Gators the next year, but at this moment, Florida was the gold standard playing an underdog Oklahoma team whose defense was run by Venables. Tebow told the television audience that Venables threw so much at the Gators they had never seen that it wasn't until halftime that Florida was able to gather its bearings and come up with a plan. The score was tied at 7 at half. Florida was up 14–7 after three quarters and held off the Sooners, 24–14.

Tebow's words resonated on Alabama's third play from scrimmage. Nickel linebacker Isaiah Simmons raced in from the wide side on a blitz. Clemson's defensive backs showed man coverage before the snap but then backed off into a zone. Pre-snap, Simmons appeared to be covering slot receiver Jerry Jeudy. Tagovailoa didn't see him blitzing until after the snap. Safety K'Von Wallace had moved over toward Jeudy, and A.J. Terrell was outside in front of DeVonta Smith.

"We were in cloud coverage," Venables said. "Something we hadn't really done going into the game."

Since it was zone coverage, Terrell was watching Tagovailoa's eyes and saw him cocking to throw Jeudy's way. Had Clemson been in man coverage, it would have been an easy completion because Jeudy had plenty of separation from Wallace and Terrell would have been locked in on Smith. But Terrell came off Smith, who tried to get a hand on Terrell. It was too late. The ball sailed behind Jeudy, and Terrell made the easy interception and saw nothing but green grass ahead. On Alabama's third play of the game, Clemson had already sent a strong message to Tagovailoa and the Tide's offense that this was going to be different from what they were used to.

"We felt like we could [get to] Tua a little bit," Swinney said. "That was a play I think we fooled him."

Alabama recovered quickly, striking on a 62-yard pass from Tagovailoa to Jeudy. And then when Clemson took possession, the Tigers looked a bit flustered. Lawrence threw high for Justyn Ross. Then John Simpson was flagged for a personal foul after tripping Quinnen Williams. On second-and-22, Clemson got 8 yards back on a throw to Trevion Thompson.

But the Tigers were still facing third-and-14 from their 21-yard line. This is normally a situation where Alabama feasts, going after a freshman quarterback and letting him know he's not playing Wake Forest anymore. Instead, what occurred was exactly what the Tigers' coaching staff envisioned: Tee Higgins running straight down the seam, right by a confused safety. Lawrence hit Higgins in stride, and Alabama didn't get him down until he reached the 17-yard line. Then another stunner: Travis Etienne taking a handoff left and finding open space before slashing and then bulling into the end zone for a 17-yard run that put Clemson up 14–7.

Alabama came right back, moving swiftly down the field on a 10-play, 75-yard touchdown drive. The extra point missed, and the score was 14–13 in Clemson's favor. The Tigers moved backward on the next drive and punted. Alabama got right back to work and seemed to have recovered just fine from Tagovailoa's pick-6.

After Josh Jacobs converted a fourth-and-1 from the Clemson 6, the Tide had first-and-goal from the 2 and then second-and-goal from the 1.

They were ready to motor into the end zone for another touchdown and then get another stop. That was what they were used to doing to everyone else. But Clemson's defense is so good that it throws offenses out of their comfort zone, and often the result is false-start penalties. Offensive lineman Jedrick Wills jumped, and the whistles blew. Running back Damien Harris threw his arms up in frustration. The Tide could not reach the end zone after moving back to the 6, and holding Bama to a field goal was a major victory for Clemson's defense. It was also the last time the Tide scored. This Alabama offense, with its superstar quarterback and the gobs of weapons around him, scored its final points of the game with 14:18 left in the second quarter.

The ensuing kickoff went out of bounds, another example of Alabama's focus and precision not being where it needed to be to match Clemson's. The Tigers started at the 35 and were quickly at midfield when Saivion Smith drew an interference penalty while trying to stick with Higgins. A running-back screen to Tavien Feaster was the perfect call against a blitz, and Feaster plowed for 26 yards. Then on third-and-5 from the 19, the offensive line provided exquisite protection for Lawrence as he waited for Higgins to run a crossing route from one end to the other. He was uncovered and picked up 14 yards and the first down. Etienne gained 4 and then a touchdown on a 1-yard run that put Clemson up 21–16 with 11:38 left in the first half.

The first sign that Saban might be headed for desperation mode came when Alabama faced a fourth-and-1 from its 35. Saban made a rare gamble by going for it instead of punting back to a Clemson offense that was starting to look unstoppable. The Tide converted on a run by Jacobs, and two more runs by Jacobs of 8 and 11 yards put Bama in good position with a first down at Clemson's 44.

On his first interception, Tagovailoa was trying to exploit Alabama's most decided matchup advantage against Clemson's defense: the Tide's explosive inside receivers against the Tigers' safeties. The long ball for a touchdown on Alabama's second possession was sinfully easy after Jeudy juked safety Tanner Muse out of his shoes with a double move. And now, down 21–16, Tagovailoa was ready to take another shot when he saw Wallace on the hash mark over Jeudy. It looked like man coverage, until it wasn't. After the snap, Wallace drifted to the middle of the field while corner Trayvon Mullen dropped into a zone instead of covering outside receiver Irv Smith man-to-man. Tagovailoa didn't recognize the coverage until it was too late. He reared back and overthrew a deep ball to Jeudy. Mullen was in the vicinity after dropping into the zone and made the easy interception.

Tebow's words earlier in the day about dealing with a Venables defense rang true. So did the feeling that Alabama's more lethal offense took more risks and put the ball in danger. In the three previous meetings with Clemson, the Tide had one turnover in 203 offensive snaps. In Round 4, they had two turnovers over their first 33 snaps.

The interception hurt, but the 46-yard return by Mullen down the sideline was a killer. One instant, Alabama had a first down in Clemson territory and was confident about taking back the lead. The next, Lawrence and Higgins and all those weapons were trotting back onto the field and inside Alabama territory.

Clemson kept its foot on the gas and was converting third downs with ease. On third-and-7 from the 31, excellent protection by the offensive line allowed Lawrence to step up in the pocket and fire to Amari Rodgers for a gain of 26. Earlier, Clemson blew up an attempted shovel pass inside the 3-yard line to force a field goal. Now the Tigers ran basically the same play to perfection, Lawrence pitching forward to Etienne for a 5-yard score.

Clemson was up 28–16 and smelling crimson blood in the water. The defensive line, even without Dexter Lawrence, started to get into the backfield. On third-and-6 from the Alabama 45, Mullen raced in on a corner blitz before Tagovailoa could get the ball off. Mullen crashed into Tagovailoa's midsection, and the ball popped out. Ross Pierschbacher was able to beat Christian Wilkins to the ball to keep Clemson from taking over in Alabama territory again. But the tone was set. Venables's defense had forced two Tagovailoa interceptions and a fumble over twenty-eight minutes of football. And on the other side, Trevor Lawrence was calmly picking apart Alabama's defense.

The Tigers ran their two-minute offense and moved from their 21 to Alabama's 16. On third-and-12 from the 18, the Tide blitzed, and Adam Choice was wide open in the left flat. If Lawrence is accurate with his throw, it's probably a touchdown to put Clemson up 35–16. He rushed it and it sailed high, forcing the Tigers to settle for a field goal that made it 31–16 instead.

Alabama got the ball back at its 25 with forty-five seconds on the clock, but Saban cut his losses after an incomplete pass and a 6-yard run by Tagovailoa. He let the clock run out, choosing to head to the locker room and regroup instead of risking a mistake that might have put his team into an even deeper hole.

Alabama had recovered from a 14-point deficit to beat Georgia in early December. And a year ago, the Tide climbed from the mat to devour a double-digit deficit and beat the Bulldogs in the national title game. And sure enough, they came out in the second half and drove right down the field. Clemson's defense held after Alabama had first down at the Tigers' 26. Backup corner Mark Fields, playing for an injured Mullen, produced a sensational pass breakup on a third-down throw to Irv Smith.

Saban sent out his field-goal team but wasn't fooling anyone. Three years earlier against Clemson, he made an audacious call for an onside kick because he knew his defense probably wasn't stopping the Tigers' offense. That paid off when Alabama recovered it and scored a touchdown soon thereafter. But this time, it probably would have been smarter for him to rely on his offense to try to pick up the six yards.

Had the Tigers been ready for that onside kick three years ago in Glendale, maybe they would have pulled away instead of losing by 5. Swinney had a sense Saban would resort to something similar to try to keep Alabama in this game. To leave no doubt, you must leave no stone unturned. So there the team was earlier in the day at the team hotel, going over fakes Saban used sixteen years ago when he was at LSU. Clemson showed one front before the snap before shifting into a different look that had the defense in perfect position to stuff holder Mac Jones.

Then, the sum of all Saban fears came to fruition: his defensive backs slipping and sliding and flailing away trying to keep Clemson's receivers in front of them. On third-and-8, Ross fought off Saivion Smith at the line, and then Smith fell backward to the turf. Safety Deionte Thompson was in position to make the tackle but couldn't get a hand on Ross as he turned upfield and outran everyone on a 74-yard touchdown dagger that put Clemson up 37–16. Smith was still writhing in pain on the turf. Clemson fans were writhing in ecstasy. This wasn't the Game of the Century. It was the Rout of the Century.

After another red-zone stop of the Tide offense, Clemson put on another aerial clinic. On third-and-12, Lawrence threw deep for Ross and Ross made a fingertip grab for a gain of 37. Ross, the Alabama kid who chose the Tigers over the Tide in part because of Clemson's coaching stability, found himself deep on the Alabama sideline after that catch. He stood for an extra beat, almost to remind the Tide what they were missing. Ross wasn't done. He made another one-handed grab near the sideline for 17 yards on third-and-9. It was as if Clemson was purposely getting to third-and-long just to make things more challenging. A year after he was playing high school ball, Ross had 12 catches against Notre Dame and Alabama for 301 yards and three touchdowns.

Christian Wilkins is emotional after Clemson's dominance of Alabama in his final collegiate game.

"Those are routine for him," Swinney said. "I mean, it's just amazing. I told Trevor, 'Could you quit throwing crappy balls so he don't have to show off like that and make some of those crazy catches?' But that's what he can do."

Lawrence, on third-and-goal from the 5, made a gorgeous throw to a leaping Higgins just over the outstretched fingertips of Mack Wilson, to a place where only Higgins could get it. Forty-four points were on the scoreboard. Clemson could've put 65 up there if it wanted to. The college football world gasped after the Tigers traveled 89 effortless yards on 12 plays. This was not fair. Two freshmen and a sophomore were making Alabama seem like it wasn't even there, and with big smiles the whole way.

"That kid cannot be nineteen years old!" play-by-play man Chris Fowler said of Lawrence. "He looks like an NFL veteran!"

Back in September, when Lawrence was showing plenty of flashes but still coming off the bench behind Kelly Bryant, he had to land a knockout punch to win the job. And now, as a freshman on the biggest stage imaginable, he had applied the knockout punch to the Crimson Tide. Alabama went across the Pacific to get its star quarterback. Clemson went across the South Carolina/Georgia border to get its guy. Now, a year after Tagovailoa engineered the unthinkable against Georgia, Lawrence was the best quarterback on the field. And it wasn't close. On January 6, 2018, Lawrence moved into his Clemson dorm room with the help of quarterbacks coach Brandon Streeter. On January 7, 2019, Lawrence distinguished himself as the best quarterback in college football. No first-year freshman had started a national championship game and won it since Oklahoma's Jamelle Holieway in 1985.

There was still an entire quarter to play. This was supposed to be nail-biting time, but instead Clemson fans partied while Alabama faithful headed to the parking lots. Venables resisted a curtain call for his stars, for the three guys who decided to come back a year earlier when everyone thought they were going pro. He kept most of his starters on the field because he wanted to keep Alabama from scoring. Venables said before and after that Alabama had the best offense he'd ever seen. Fourteen years before, Venables's Oklahoma team played Southern Cal for a national title in the Orange Bowl. The Trojans looked like an NFL team that night in a scorching 55–19 victory, led by a cast of elite offensive playmakers that included Reggie Bush, Matt Leinart, LenDale White, Dwayne Jarrett, Steve Smith and Dominique Byrd. Venables said this Crimson Tide offense surpassed even that USC juggernaut.

"This is a special performance after a special year," he said. "This is a great legacy that these guys lived out, and I can't thank them enough. I think your character and leadership are revealed in those moments. It's easy to say, but that's what it comes down to: a sheer will to win and compete and not be discouraged or not to be denied, and to find a way."

The Tigers held the ball for the final ten minutes with their offensive reserves in the game, churning out 94 yards and coming darned close to reaching the end zone again. In 166 games at Alabama, Saban had never trailed by more than 20 points. Only out of Clemson's generosity did he keep from getting beaten by 35 and seeing the Tigers hang half a hundred on his Crimson Tide.

Two years earlier, the feeling of beating Alabama was surreal and wonderful and dreamlike in part because Clemson had not yet done it. Tears were abundant that night on the sideline and in the stands in Tampa. They had done it with one second left on the clock, and it felt like at least a small miracle. At halftime of that game, Clemson was down 14–0 and on the verge of getting run out of Raymond James Stadium. Swinney told his guys in the locker room that somehow, some way they were going to get it done. He didn't know how, but they were going to find a way.

This demolition was confirmation of what Swinney and his staff felt going in. No, none of them were thinking they'd win by 28. But they were thinking this time they were good enough to make a convincing case. Good enough to leave no doubt. Good enough to be the first 15-0 team in forever without having to rely on a last-minute drive. As the final seconds ticked away and co–offensive coordinator Tony Elliott made his way from the coaches' box down to the field to join the celebration, he yelled, "Best ever, baby! Two out of three!" Elliott and the Tigers beat Notre Dame and Alabama by a combined score of 74–19.

"I know we're not supposed to be here," Swinney said during the victory celebration as the confetti fell. "We're just little ole Clemson and I'm not supposed to be here. But we are. And I am."

Where the celebration two years before was unbridled joy, this one had a bit of an edge. The defense laughed at the thought that losing Dexter Lawrence would be a big deal or the notion that the safeties were the weak link who would be exploited. The offense scoffed at the notion that the line couldn't protect Lawrence or open holes for Etienne.

"Where are the fools who said we couldn't block those guys?" offensive line coach Robbie Caldwell yelled to a group of media as he walked from the field to the locker room. His offensive line didn't allow one sack, and as it turned out, Quinnen Williams was human after all.

The three defensive linemen who came back to finish the job—Christian Wilkins, Clelin Ferrell and Austin Bryant—soaked in their final moments in Clemson uniforms. Wilkins and Dexter Lawrence were walking off the field when they heard the band playing the alma mater and stopped to sing. Wilkins began weeping.

Trevor Lawrence was one of the first players to the locker room, but he quickly came back out to greet his teammates as they filed in. To each, he gave a hug while saying, "I love you."

In 2015 and 2016, Clemson brought its own guts to push Alabama to the edge and finally knock off the Tide. In 2018, Swinney and the Tigers brought their own sledgehammer. A superhuman effort is no longer necessary for Clemson to prevail over college football's Death Star. Not just chip away at it but blow the dang thing to bits. "There was a lot of talk about 'the best ever' all year long," Swinney said. "We were never in that conversation. Tonight there was no doubt."

Two days before the championship game, this writer had a conversation with former Alabama running back Shaun Alexander. Before he became an NFL star, Alexander was with the Crimson Tide when Swinney was

Trevor Lawrence gets his hands on the national championship trophy.

an assistant in Tuscaloosa. After Clemson had laid waste to Alabama, Alexander's words from two days earlier resonated. He had been asked to describe Swinney's style and said this: "We're cut from the same mold: We're going to smile, but we're going to murder you. Not everybody has to grind your teeth and cuss everybody out to cut you alive."

Swinney has been dreaming big since he got the job ten years ago as a receivers coach who'd never even run an offense, let alone a team. More recently, he taught everyone it was possible to play with Alabama. Then he taught everyone it was possible to beat them. Now, the biggest step of all: Clemson existing as precisely the type of cold-blooded killer Alabama has been for so long.

In the wake of so many landmark moments before this one, Swinney kept saying the best was yet to come. Now it's easy to see what he's talking about, given that it seems this startlingly young offense is just getting started. And though the defense loses a load of talent from the group that held Alabama scoreless over the final 44:18, Venables and his staff have plenty of elite talent ready to elevate.

Five days after a glorious night at a place Swinney called "wherever-the-heck California we are," five days after he told Saban "see ya next year,"

After putting off the NFL a year earlier, Christian Wilkins goes out on top.

Swinney took the stage at a stadium celebration that followed a parade honoring the 1981 champs, the 2016 champs and now the 2018 champs. A while earlier, he'd done a short interview with a TV station and was asked how it felt. "It's surreal," he said. "Can't wait to do it again."

Now he was in front of the microphone in front of the sea of orange and purple, a man of the people who had promised and delivered. After they lost to Alabama that first time, he said it wouldn't be long before they'd be back. After they beat Alabama the first time, he said the best was still yet to come. And after that agonizing night in New Orleans, he said it wasn't over.

And now, he wanted to make one thing clear.

"The 2018 team is absolutely the best team ever," he said. "Drop the mic. The best team ever."

Swinney, forty-nine, was wrong about one thing. This team was never on any ROY Bus or even close to it. Going all the way out to Northern California made more sense in hindsight: it was a Golden Gate to a Dabo Dynasty, and the Tigers were on the Destroy Bus as they coasted through.

EPILOGUE

Normally, Terry Don Phillips is too nervous to watch the games live. He wakes up the next day, his wife tells him the result and he watches the replay on DVR, somewhat comforted by knowing who won. That's the routine.

But after midnight on January 9, 2017, after the ball settled into Hunter Renfrow's grasp with 59 minutes and 59 seconds gone, Tricia Phillips decided to break protocol. She ran upstairs in their Seneca home, shook her husband awake and told him he had to watch this live.

So as they sat in front of the television and witnessed the uproarious celebration of the national title, the vanquishing of mighty Alabama, eventually the microphone went to Dabo Swinney, and he celebrated the man who hired him. Then husband and wife were so excited that they decided to watch the entire game and didn't get to bed until around 5:00 a.m.

"Ended up staying up pretty much all night," Phillips said. "You couldn't lay down and not think about it."

Two years later, when Clemson played Alabama for the fourth year in a row, Phillips could have watched the first half, gone to bed at halftime and slept soundly knowing the Tigers were ahead comfortably. They had another parade five days later to celebrate the 44–16 demolition of Alabama for the program's second national title in three years.

But for this observer, a scene from that first celebration two years ago at Death Valley still lingered and stirred. Once the parade was over and everyone moved into the stadium so Swinney and others could speak, the head coach immediately stepped down from the stage and went directly from Point A to Point TDP.

Anyone who saw their long embrace would have to agree it was the most indelible, powerful moment of the day. A coach at the peak of his profession paying an emotional tribute to the man who had the guts and the vision to believe in him when almost no one else did. Phillips's wife captured the moment with a photo.

"When you walk through some rough waters with someone, you either like the person you're walking with or you don't," Phillips said later that day. "I think he knows what side of the line I was on."

When Phillips made the decision to step away in August 2012, Clemson football hadn't achieved enough to bring much celebration of his retirement. Yes, the Tigers had won the ACC in 2011 for the first time in forever. But they were also a few months removed from a 70–33 Orange Bowl debacle against West Virginia. They had also suffered a fifth straight loss to South Carolina the previous November. Let's put it this way: had they arranged for a parade to celebrate that season, that January seven years ago, you could have fit everyone into the Esso Club with some room to spare.

The jury was still out on Swinney at that point. Thus, the jury was still out on Phillips and the highly unconventional decisions he made in 2008— one to promote a receivers coach to interim head coach after Tommy Bowden's mid-October departure and the next to give him the job for good after he went 4-2 with not one of the wins coming over a team that would finish ranked.

Maybe Gary Patterson or Troy Calhoun or Bud Foster or some other coach on Phillips's list would have won big had Phillips made a safer play. But would anyone else speak to Clemson fans and unite them the way Swinney did and does? Would anyone else on the planet seem as made to preside over a stadium celebration the way Swinney has twice in the past three years?

This is what Phillips envisioned when he parted with Bowden and saw Swinney as much more a man of the people who could do more than just recruit and coach receivers. He knew there'd be some struggle, but he probably didn't think he'd have to deal with such unrest just two years after promoting Swinney.

When things go wrong quickly with a head coach from the previous staff, as they did in 2010 when Clemson finished 6-7, the fan base and the heavy hitters are going to be quicker to call for change and demand answers. It's not necessarily fair, but it's reality. So even after the ACC division title in

Swinney's first full season, the dip in his second season brought extreme emotions. And as a vocal fringe element rallied support for billboards of protest, they weren't going after the head coach as much as they were going after the man who hired the head coach.

Phillips recalled an article that associate AD Billy D'Andrea showed him back in 2010 that said the Swinney hire was "laughable."

"A lot of people at that time thought it was an idiotic hire," he said. "And I could see how some people would feel that way. I knew there would be some push-back and apathy, because he didn't have the credentials."

It wasn't just assorted fans who were angry. Powerful people, including some trustees, were bringing heat. It was so tense that, after the loss to South Carolina in 2010, Swinney thought Phillips was going to fire him when Kathleen Swinney told him his boss was waiting in his office late that night. As it turned out, Phillips surprised him by telling him he was more convinced than ever he was the right guy. Phillips said President Jim Barker stood strong behind his convictions, never vacillating in his support of Phillips and Swinney amid all the scrutiny.

At various points back then, Phillips would tell his head coach, "If this doesn't work out, I'll come help you pack up your office. And then you can come help me pack up mine."

Phillips, years later: "We were very close during that period of time, because you had to be close. You had to watch your backside."

Phillips lives five miles from campus but has kept to himself and watched it all blossom from a distance. His successor, Dan Radakovich, has presided over a much-needed modernization of the athletics department with new, aggressive approaches to facilities and fundraising and communications. The administration, including President Jim Clements and the Board of Trustees, is all-in with football and has achieved extraordinary synergy and camaraderie up and down the chain of command.

The infrastructure of the football program and athletics department and everything around Clemson is almost unrecognizable from the days when Phillips occupied that corner office in the McFadden Building. The entire school, not just the football program, seems to be taking that next step.

But this step wouldn't be possible without that first step in 2008. The step of promoting the man who is now the face and the voice and the thrust of an entire culture.

When Phillips announced he was walking away in August 2012, there was no grand celebration. There wasn't much of a celebration at all beyond those in the athletics department who wished him well. At that moment,

Dabo Swinney and Terry Don Phillips, January 2017. *By Tricia Phillips.*

Clemson under Swinney was 29-19. Since, the Tigers are 87-11 with two national championships and more trophies than they can count.

During the more recent stadium celebration, Swinney again credited Phillips. Two years before, on the stage in Tampa when pulses were still racing after that 35–31 thriller, Swinney delivered full-throated, passionate recognition of Phillips on national television. Then he did it again a few days later inside the stadium when the fans came to celebrate the school's first national title since 1981.

That first one meant the most to Phillips. He was out of sight and out of mind to almost everyone. Almost.

"Words really can't describe how I felt," Phillips said. "That's a very, very special moment in my life. And for Tricia, because she had to go through a little bit of the heartache we all went through. We're all a lot smarter retrospectively. The people that had some discontent, they can see the history and recognize how far we have come and recognize it was a good decision. But I thought it was a good decision then. I never thought it was a bad decision. Not to pat myself on the back, but…"

The man who walked quietly into the sunset gets to bask in the light.

WHAT THEY WERE SAYING

Excerpts from the work filed by national columnists in the wake of Clemson's stunning dismantling of Alabama.

IT WAS COMPLETE DOMINANCE—AND not a fluke. Coaches love to talk about how much more difficult it is to stay on top than to get there. The Tigers climbed to No. 1 two years ago with a thrilling 35–31 victory over the Tide. It took a once-in-a-generation quarterback in Deshaun Watson to lead Clemson to a touchdown with :01 remaining on the clock. Last year, when Clemson succumbed meekly to Alabama 24–6 in a playoff semifinal, the Tigers' second loss to the Tide in three seasons, it seemed that a gap still existed between the two programs. There is no gap, not anymore. Clemson has won two of the past four national championships. Alabama has won the other two. Clemson beat Alabama to win its two. Alabama won a close game and a rout. Clemson won a close game and a rout. It's safe to say that, from a historical viewpoint, the Tigers have proved that they are every bit the power that Alabama is. That's Clemson, long known as the football school in the basketball conference, a program known a generation ago for regular trips to NCAA jail, that sits atop the college football world and routed two blue bloods to do it.

—Ivan Maisel, ESPN

SO WHILE THE TIDE and the Tigers spent most of the 2018 season separating themselves from the rest of college football, Swinney separated himself from Saban. At least for one magical night. We may have to rethink the whole Alabama-Clemson nouveau rivalry. Suddenly, it's Clemson becoming the first major-college team to finish 15-0 in 121 years. Suddenly, it's the Tigers who have won two of the last three national championships. Suddenly, it's Clemson with the best overall team on the planet.

Suddenly, it's Alabama looking for answers…the biggest one being how to stop Lawrence.…You have the feeling this series isn't over by a long shot. The teams have now played four straight years. The point differential is nine—in Clemson's favor. Alabama will be back, but this time it will be in a rare position…chasing down Clemson to get to another championship. At least that's the way it seems. Lawrence was among 20 true freshmen who played for Clemson this season. That's the most at the school since 1982. The seniors set a college football record—winning their 55th game. Clemson will likely end as the No. 1 team in the AP Top 25 for the second time in three years despite never being No. 1 at any point during the season. For the Tide, Sweet Home Alabama is a 2,300-mile flight into an offseason of uncertainty. The uncertainty: How the hell are we going to beat Clemson?
—Dennis Dodd, CBSSports.com

"WHEN DID YOU FEEL that you had broken their will?" ESPN's Rece Davis asked Clemson head coach Dabo Swinney on the championship podium after the game. Davis later asked starting quarterback Trevor Lawrence, "When did you feel that you guys had complete and total control of the game?" These are the types of questions you would like to ask a boa constrictor about the small mammal it just strangled and ate. For a decade, Alabama has been the boa constrictor; Monday, the most dominant college football program of the century was relegated to the role of the deceased mouse.…Clemson is now the national champion, and its victory seems bigger than a one-year reign atop the sport. For the first time in years, college football's pecking order has shifted. Alabama can no longer lay sole claim to being the preeminent program in the nation.…I've never seen Alabama look like this. Nobody has. Of the 167 games Saban has coached at Alabama, this was tied for the second-worst defensive performance and the 10th-worst offensive performance in terms of scoring. Bama appeared shook. Bama never appears shook. The scary thing is there's probably more where this came from. Some of the biggest plays Monday night were made by true freshmen, on passes from Lawrence to wide receiver Justyn Ross....Saban has now coached in eight national championship games and won six. The only two losses have come against Clemson. And these losses haven't seemed like *LSU 9, Alabama 6* or *Ole Miss 43, Alabama 37* or the fabled Kick-Six. The Tigers are beating Alabama because they are every bit as good as Alabama, week after week, year after year.

—Rodger Sherman, The Ringer

WHAT CLEMSON DID TO a Nick Saban–coached Alabama team Monday night at Levi's Stadium was absolutely unprecedented, and it's worth savoring if you were among the delirious folks in orange who found their way west from the Piedmont for their team's first game of 2019. But on the flight back to South Carolina, while reliving every little tidbit that will make so many memories for the Tigers, get giddy over this, Clemson: Who's to say this won't happen again? The national title game was, in fact, a blowout, because the final was Clemson 44, Alabama 16. Blowouts are supposed to be boring. But blowouts don't happen to Alabama. So this wasn't boring. This, the fourth straight College Football Playoff meeting between these programs, was revelatory. And it was staggering. Staggering because of the talent Clemson rolled out to execute it. Staggering because of who it came against. And staggering because so many of these characters could come back to this same stage and do this all again....But whatever frustration Saban felt had to be replaced with some measure of admiration, even begrudgingly, for how the Clemson players, who are excellent, executed Clemson's game plan, which was superbly. The two previous national championship games between these teams were head-spinning, down-to-the-final-possession affairs, five points in favor of Alabama in 2016, four points in favor of Clemson in 2017. What amounted to a beatdown was the Crimson Tide's 24–6 victory in last year's semifinals, and that game felt closer. The way the Tigers managed the matter of Monday night was completely different.

—Barry Svrluga, the *Washington Post*

REMEMBER THIS MOMENT, THIS time and place and undeniable paradigm shift in college football. All at the hands of the generational quarterback— and a generational ass-kicking. "Trevor Lawrence," Clemson wide receiver Justyn Ross said, "has no ceiling." Welcome to a new world in college football, everyone. A decade of the inevitable is over after Clemson's 44–

16 dismantling of longtime king Alabama in the national championship game. Lawrence, Clemson's 19-year-old true freshman wunderkind of a quarterback, has changed the way we look at who owns the game. Ding, dong, the witch, finally, is dead. The second generational quarterback Swinney recruited [Lawrence] then stood tall at the top of the mountain and left no doubt who is leading and who is following. Moments after the final seconds mercifully melted away for the most dominant dynasty in the modern era—after Clemson road-graded Alabama by holding the ball for the final 10:02 with a "you may as well get used to this" drive—Deshaun Watson was circling the field at Levi's Stadium, looking for someone to hug. "It was beautiful, it was perfect," Watson said when asked about this championship season compared to his....As impressive as Clemson's clobbering of Alabama was, there's a compelling reality that still remains: This program is built to win for the long haul. The only thing that kept Clemson from backing up its 2017 national title the next season was average quarterback play in the College Football Playoff semifinal loss to Alabama. Then Lawrence arrived, and he was so good from the moment he stepped on campus as a midterm enrollee that there was little doubt where the season was headed. It didn't take long for him to beat out starter Kelly Bryant, and it was a short leap to reaffirming what the staff had known for years: He would change the way people looked at Clemson football....Moments after the championship rout, Swinney stood on the stage at Levi's Stadium and announced that Clemson would enjoy this national championship for a couple of days before the first team meeting for 2019 on Friday. That was the first team meeting Lawrence attended in 2018, the first time he met his new teammates, and three months before he threw his first pass in pads during spring practice. "This one might be a little different this time around," Lawrence said with a smile. It will be his team this Friday. The generational quarterback standing on top of the college football mountain. With the paradigm shift in college football.

—Matt Hayes, Bleacher Report

IN WINNING MONDAY, SWINNEY was the man with all the answers while Saban (of all people) was watching his team self-destruct—turnovers, penalties, blown coverages, special-teams snafus, red-zone futility. This was a shocking woodshed beating, with the Tigers executing like the confident, cold-blooded machine that so often has been Alabama. It was the worst loss of Saban's tenure in Tuscaloosa, and the worst any Saban-coached team has suffered since a 45–16 loss to Georgia while the coach at LSU in 2004. Behind this powerhouse performance, Clemson becomes just the 10th team since the AP poll era began in 1936 to win at least two national championships in a three-year span. The rest of the list: Alabama, Florida, USC, Nebraska, Miami, Oklahoma, Notre Dame, Army and Minnesota. In the process, Swinney has surpassed celebrated coaches like Steve Spurrier, Lou Holtz, Bob Stoops and Vince Dooley—they all won one title. Swinney now moves alongside Bobby Bowden, Joe Paterno and Ara Parseghian with two. And guess what? At age 49, with a superstar quarterback who will play two more years in an orange uniform, Dabo is nowhere near finished.

—Pat Forde, Yahoo.com

CLEMSON'S UNDERDOG SWAGGER IS officially dead. It has been replaced by a new mystique as the program that didn't just erase the Alabama gap, but instead vaporized it. And as the first modern college team to ever go 15-0, Clemson's locker room was buzzing with talk that they could go down as the best college football team of all time. "Coach Swinney has been talking all year about leave no doubt, and obviously two years ago we were very happy to win, great way to win one, but it comes down to a couple plays," co-offensive coordinator Jeff Scott said, referring to Clemson's epic 35–31 victory on a last-second touchdown in Tampa. "That was the challenge coach Swinney gave our team. Just play our best four quarters and if we do that we'll leave no doubt." Ultimately, where this Clemson team ranks in history is not as relevant as the staggering manner in which it ran Alabama off the field. A bunch of freshmen playmakers humiliated the Crimson Tide's defense at every turn. And even without Dexter Lawrence, Clemson's best defensive lineman, the Tigers still turned quarterback Tua Tagovailoa into a gaffe machine, including a tone-setting pick-6 on Alabama's first drive, another horrible interception and multiple empty trips inside the 10-yard line….But the most important point that will carry into the offseason is that this performance wasn't a fluke, nor is Clemson a one-off. When Alabama lost to the Tigers in 2016, the national takeaway was that Deshaun Watson's one-of-a-kind brilliance to win that game probably couldn't be replicated, especially if Saban stuck around. But now, that argument is done forever. Clemson, as of today, is the more complete program. And that isn't just about players like Lawrence, who made elite third-down throws while avoiding the mistakes that Tagovailoa made. It was a maligned Clemson offensive line that simply manhandled the vaunted Alabama defensive front.

It was Clemson's receivers leaving Alabama defenders in the dust. And it was about an Alabama coaching staff that simply got dominated at every turn. "I just have a feeling that I didn't do a very good job for our team, with our team, giving them the best opportunity to be successful," Saban said. Alabama can still win championships as long as Saban coaches, but the earth moved underneath his feet Monday night. Swinney is the new king of college football.

—Dan Wolken, *USA Today*

THE TIGERS' WIN WAS a statement about the future of college football as much as the present. When the confetti shower was over, the night felt like the start of something even bigger than a single national championship party. It was a moment that had been 10 years in the making....In the fourth straight playoff meeting between Alabama and Clemson, Ross and Lawrence certainly did tip the scales in the Tigers' favor. On a third-and-eight play midway through the third quarter, Ross caught a ball on the right sideline and took it 74 yards for a touchdown to put Clemson up by 21. On Clemson's next drive, Ross batted a ball to himself for a 37-yard catch on a third-and-12 play. He later made a one-handed grab along the right sideline for a 17-yard gain on third-and-nine. That helped set up a five-yard Lawrence-to-Higgins touchdown that confirmed the Tigers wouldn't only beat Alabama. They would *crush* Alabama. And now Swinney, the former Alabama walk-on receiver who got a seven-week audition 10 years ago, has done exactly what he envisioned. He has built Clemson into a program that expects to play for the national title every year. "To be successful, you have to have a vision for what you want to do and a clear plan," Swinney said as he walked to the team bus after the championship victory. "And then you can't be afraid to fail. You've got to keep getting up. That's what we've done for 10 years." Then he walked on, planning already for the next 10.

—Andy Staples, *Sports Illustrated*

WHERE WERE YOU THE night the earth under college football shifted? At what point did you realize Monday night that Clemson was not just going to win the fourth installment of its Playoff rivalry with Alabama, but that Dabo Swinney also would hand Nick Saban the most lopsided defeat of his 12-year tenure? Even now, however many hours or days after the fact you're reading this column, how jarring is it still to see the words Clemson 44, Alabama

16? "It feels like a dream," fifth-year Tigers receiver Hunter Renfrow said in his team's Levi's Stadium locker room after capturing his second national championship in three seasons. We live in a different world than the one we woke up to Monday morning. There are now two superpowers in college football. Alabama has lorded over the sport for most of the past decade, capturing five national titles along the way. There were occasional interlopers, like Jameis Winston's Florida State team, Ezekiel Elliott's Ohio State squad and, yes, Renfrow's Clemson Tigers just two seasons ago. The dynasty didn't die with one nightmarish meltdown. Alabama will still carry every expectation to reach this same night in New Orleans a year from now. But Clemson has staked its claim once and for all as being every bit as much of a giant. Swinney's program holds the same exact record as Alabama—55-4—since 2015, and his Tigers have now slayed the Tide twice in three seasons. So now, it's Alabama 2, Clemson 2. Maybe they'll meet for a rubber match next year in New Orleans, with Tua and Trevor reprising their roles under center and Swinney and Saban holding yet another joint news conference the day before the game. Either way, their legacies are now intertwined. Saban built the dynasty that came to define a decade of college football. Swinney built the foil that finally solved it. And now, especially after three-time national champion Urban Meyer's retirement, they go forward as the undisputed kings of their sport. We now live in a world where Alabama has an equal.

—Stewart Mandel, The Athletic

THE DOWNSIDE OF BEING a titanic, multigenerational behemoth like Alabama is that any institution that builds so much has a lot to lose. Swinney has managed to match Saban as a recruiter and tactician, but in a program that's still very much on the rise. And it is, crucially, a program that's evolved to the point that it can beat Alabama, not just a team that caught lightning in a bottle. For instance, Auburn went 14-0 in 2010 with Cam Newton under center, but went 8-5 the year before he arrived and returned to 8-5 the year after he went to the NFL. Clemson, on the other hand, has turned over nearly its entire roster over the course of its four straight playoff appearances, demonstrating depth to match Alabama's. On Monday, the Tigers pushed Bama down the Slip 'N Slide without starting defensive tackle Dexter Lawrence, who was suspended for the postseason for a PED violation, and behind a true freshman quarterback, Trevor Lawrence, who didn't open the season as the starter. Lawrence is the third different quarterback to take

Clemson to the playoff in the past three years. And another top-10 recruiting class is on the way. Clemson is built to last, in other words. Over the past half decade, nobody's been able to tweak Saban's nose quite like Swinney; on Monday night, he just about pulled it clean off. And there's no end in sight.
—Michael Baumann, The Ringer

ABOUT THE AUTHOR

Larry Williams with family. *By Heidi Williams.*

arry Williams has covered Clemson football on a daily basis since early 2004, when he joined the *Post & Courier* of Charleston, South Carolina. In 2008, he moved to Tigerillustrated.com. In 2007, he was named South Carolina Sportswriter of the Year by the National Sportscasters and Sportswriters Association. In 2011, he and Travis Haney coauthored the book *Classic Clashes of the Carolina-Clemson Football Rivalry: A State of Disunion.* He released *The Danny Ford Years at Clemson: Romping and Stomping* in 2012 and *Clemson Tough: Guts and Glory Under Dabo Swinney* in 2016. He lives in the Clemson area with his wife and two daughters, and in his spare time, he enjoys reading the book *Dark Places* while improving his tan at Florida State games.

Visit us at
www.historypress.com